Wakefield Press

The Third Brother

Penny Matthews has written more than thirty books for children, as well as books on subjects as diverse as Australian colonial cookery and the novels of Thomas Hardy. Country life has often featured in her work, most notably in *A Year on Our Farm*, the Children's Book Council of Australia's 2003 Book of the Year: Early Childhood. Her young adult novel *A Girl Like Me*, based on her research into the murder of a teenage girl in rural South Australia in 1902, won the 2011 Davitt Award for Children's and Young Adult Literature.

By the same author

The Sea Dog
Heart of Magic
A Girl Like Me
Eureka Boys
The Nellie Stories

Picture books

A Year on Our Farm
Something About Water
Show Day
The Gift
One Night

The Third Brother

a story of family, and war

Penny Matthews

Wakefield
Press

Wakefield Press
16 Rose Street
Mile End
South Australia 5031
www.wakefieldpress.com.au

First published 2017

Copyright © Penny Matthews, 2017

All rights reserved. This book is copyright. Apart from any fair dealing for the purposes of private study, research, criticism or review, as permitted under the Copyright Act, no part may be reproduced without written permission. Enquiries should be addressed to the publisher.

Cover designed by Liz Nicholson, designBITE
Text designed and typeset by Clinton Ellicott, Wakefield Press

National Library of Australia Cataloguing-in-Publication entry

Creator:	Matthews, Penny, 1945– , author.
Title:	The third brother: a story of family, and war / Penny Matthews.
ISBN:	978 1 74305 425 3 (paperback).
Notes:	Includes index.
Subjects:	Murrie, Glen. Australia. Royal Australian Air Force – Airmen – Biography. Bomber pilots – Australia – Biography. World War, 1939–1945 – Participation, Australian. Men – Australia – Biography.
Dewey Number:	940.544092

For David, Bruce and Gwenyth,
and for their children and grandchildren
and great-grandchildren

Contents

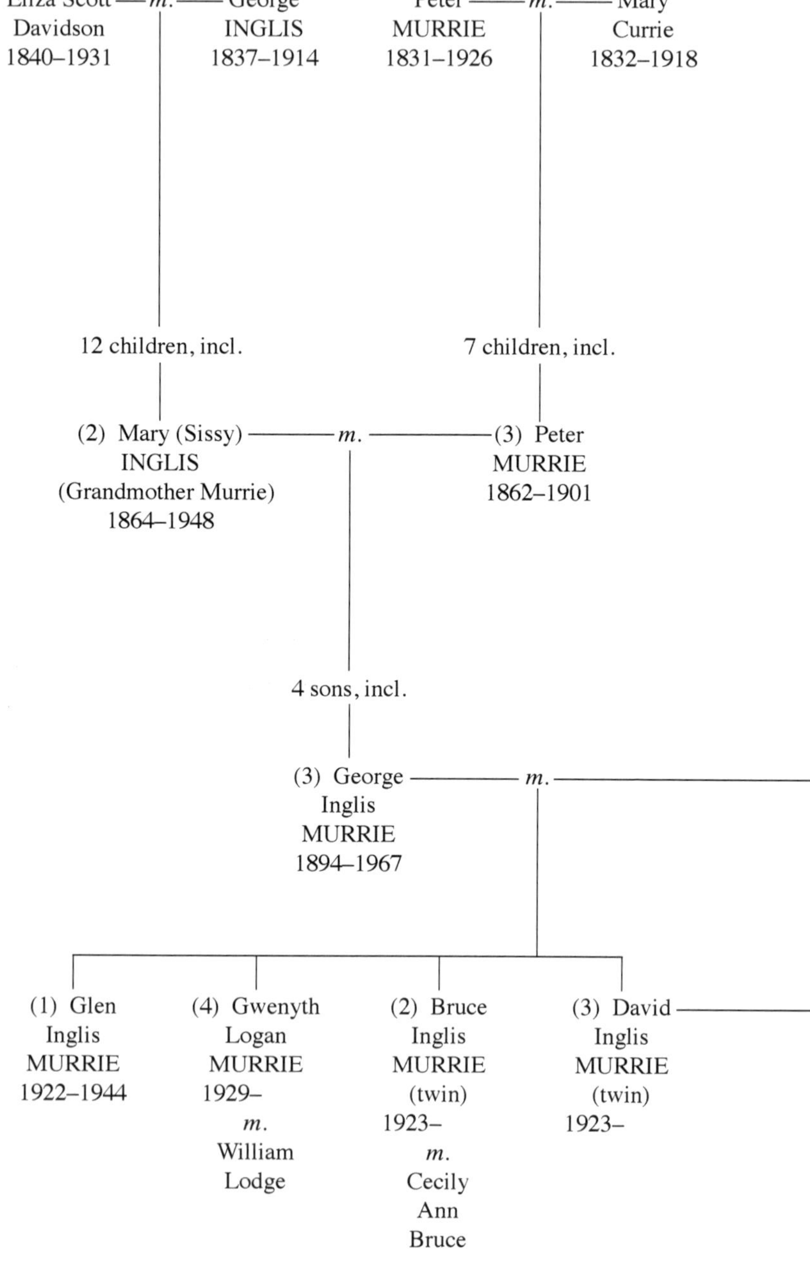
Eliza Scott Davidson 1840–1931
m.
George INGLIS 1837–1914
Peter MURRIE 1831–1926
m.
Mary Currie 1832–1918
12 children, incl.
7 children, incl.
(2) Mary (Sissy) INGLIS (Grandmother Murrie) 1864–1948
m.
(3) Peter MURRIE 1862–1901
4 sons, incl.
(3) George Inglis MURRIE 1894–1967
m.
(1) Glen Inglis MURRIE 1922–1944
(4) Gwenyth Logan MURRIE 1929–
m.
William Lodge
(2) Bruce Inglis MURRIE (twin) 1923–
m.
Cecily Ann Bruce
(3) David Inglis MURRIE (twin) 1923–

The Family

Pulteney Malcolm MURRAY 1817–1879
m.
(i) Mary Ann Scott 1820–1856 (9 children; 5 died in infancy)
m.
(ii) Elizabeth VIGAR 1838–1925
12 children, incl.
(4) Ernest Albert MURRAY 1864–1905
m.
Emily Mary Alice (Em) LOGAN (Grandmother Murray) 1868–1961
(2) Mary Ann MURRAY 1859–1929
m.
David SHANNON 1855–1900
1 son (died in infancy) 4 daughters, incl.
(3) Lulu Logan MURRAY 1897–1997
11 children, incl.
(4) Emily Winifred SHANNON 1883–1966
m.
William Thomas VIGAR 1879–1955
m.
(3) Elizabeth Barbara Shannon VIGAR 1921–2008
(1) Kathleen Mary Shannon VIGAR 1914–2003
m.
John Murray
(2) Leonard William Shannon VIGAR 1916–1991
m.
Marguerite Ramsay

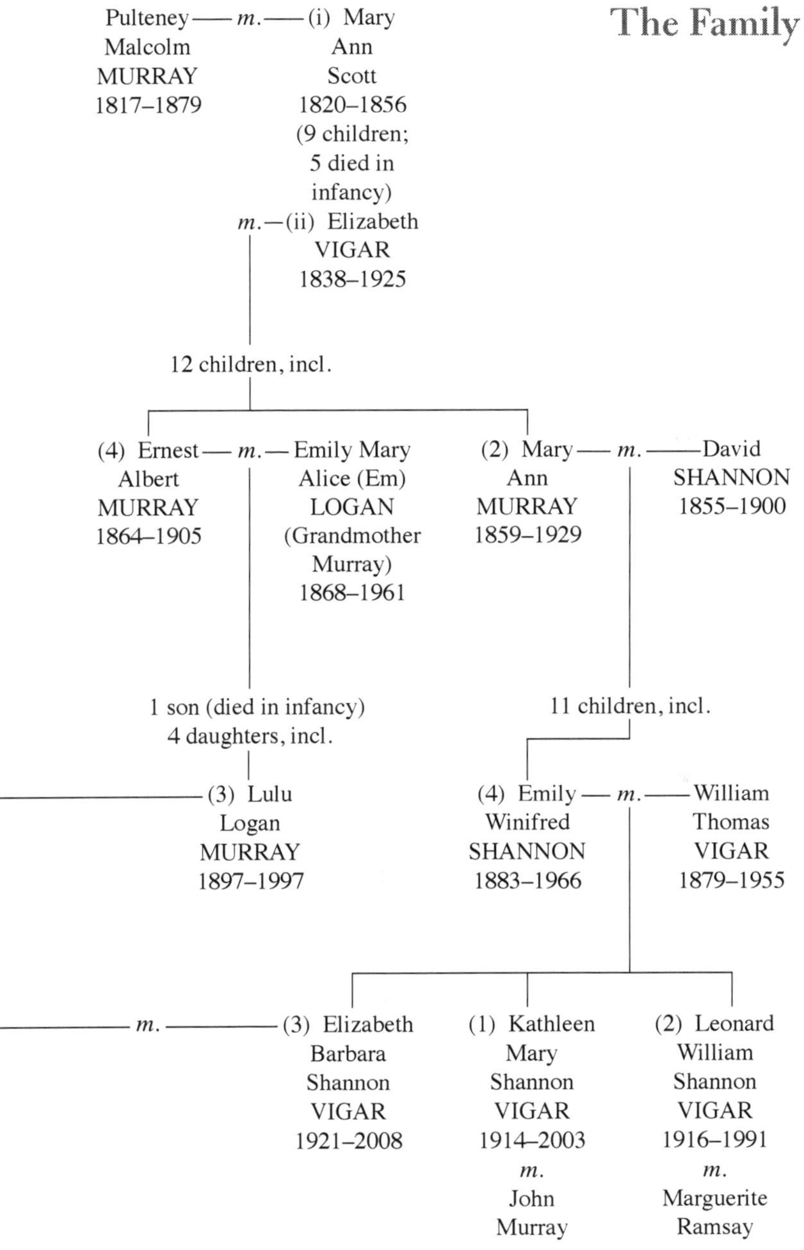

‘If a story begins with finding, it must end with searching.’
– Penelope Fitzgerald, *The Blue Flower*

Chapter 1

Finding

Our car slows down at the gates, turns left, accelerates up the winding bare-earth driveway, stops at the front of the house. The handbrake grates up. Three car doors creak open. From the back seat, I probe with my sandalled feet for a safe foothold.

We are here, my brother and I, because our mother is not well. We are aware that something has happened: at home there is an unsettling air of false reassurance. We don't know what's wrong, exactly. What we do know is that we are to stay here at Ravenswood with our aunt and uncle. Our father is even now getting a suitcase out of the boot. It's our mother's suitcase, the stippled cream fibre one with a tattered travel sticker on it, blue and white with a big black initial R. Inside it are our small bits of clothing – pants and singlets, shirts and shorts and dresses ironed and neatly folded, our toothbrushes and a tin of tooth powder.

I am holding my teddy bear and wearing my blue gingham dress with the white collar. My mother made it on our old black-and-gold Wertheim sewing machine, and it's my favourite. It is lightly starched, and it ties behind with a sash. The back of the skirt is damp and crumpled from my sitting in the warmth of the car. I try to pull it straight.

The screen door opens and our cousins come out,

followed by their father, David Murrie, our Uncle David. Our cousins, Nicky and Anne, stand and stare at us, mouths open. In the summer of 1952 they are still babies. I am six, and my brother, twenty months older, has just turned eight.

Uncle David and my father shake hands, and my uncle picks up the case. He says something in his deep voice: my father replies. They are turned away from us so we can't hear what they are saying. My uncle is dark-haired, dark-eyed, tanned, impossibly tall. He is the tallest man I know. He wears a khaki shirt with the sleeves torn out, so he looks like a workman. My father is wearing cuffed grey flannel trousers and his tan herringbone tweed sports jacket with shiny woven leather buttons. Standing next to my uncle, he looks less himself, slightly diminished. The sunburnt V of his neck is hidden by a shirt buttoned up to the top, and a striped tie. Usually he only dresses like this when he goes to sheep sales. I know that today he isn't going to a sheep sale.

My brother and I stand and look down at the ground. We have been to our aunt and uncle's house many times before, but today it's unfamiliar because our mother isn't here. Without her we feel shy and exposed.

The screen door opens again. Our Aunt Elizabeth comes up to us, and suddenly everything is all right. She puts her hand on the side of my head and presses it gently into her hip. Her kind eyes shine behind her glasses. Her fine light brown hair is held back on one side by a bobby pin, and she wears a red-striped seersucker dress with three nappy pins hanging from the collar in a small chain.

There is nobody kinder than my aunt, nobody so gentle and tranquil and sweet-tempered. We love her second only to our mother, and even more than our father, whose younger sister she is. We are both in awe of our father, not because he is cruel or unkind – he isn't – but because there is something aloof and solitary about him. The deep love he has for our mother has never extended to us, or not in any way that we can see. Our relationship is one of mutual respect. My brother and I share a tacit understanding that our father would be deeply embarrassed if we were to show him physical affection.

Although we have lived our entire lives with our father, we have no name for him. Others ignorantly refer to him as our daddy. Once, when we were holidaying at the beach and our father had to go back to our farm because it was a bad bushfire day, our grandmother, his mother, instructed us to 'kiss Daddy goodbye', an occasion that was painful and humiliating for all three of us. We don't do kissing, and certainly not kissing as prescribed social ritual.

When our father leaves, which he does very soon, he says goodbye to our uncle and aunt, but not to us. I am aware that farewells, with their potential for awkward emotion, are not necessary, and I feel a certain pride at our dignity and reticence. At a deep unspoken level, we three – my father, my brother and I – all understand each other.

My uncle picks up my small girl cousin, Anne, who has toddled up to him and is supporting herself against his knee. He swings her into the air and on to his shoulders so that she shrieks with fear and joy.

I hug my teddy bear.

Our car snakes off down the driveway, followed by a low haze of brown dust. We watch it until it reaches the gate, turns right, and disappears. Is our father going to take our mother to hospital now? Will she be going to the hospital in

Mount Pleasant, or, more seriously, to somewhere in Town? (Adelaide is always called Town and never The City.) But we don't ask.

'Come along, Miss Muffet,' my aunt says, taking my hand. She bends down to my brother and ruffles his hair. 'You too, Windy Bill.' She doesn't embarrass him by taking his hand: she understands that at eight he is too grown-up for this. Her voice always sounds as if it is about to bubble into laughter. She cannot be much older than thirty (I now realise), but laughter lines are already etched into her face.

We go inside for home-made Anzac biscuits and lemon cordial. The biscuits are kept in a glass jar with a transfer of pink roses on the lid. The house smells faintly and comfortably of milk and nappies.

That evening we have rabbit stew for dinner. I have never had rabbit stew before. There are six of us at the kitchen table: my aunt and uncle; my brother and me; Nicky, a sturdy, dark-eyed, fair-haired child, almost three years old; and toddler Anne, who is in a high chair. In time three more children will be born, another girl and then two more boys.

We stay with Uncle David and Aunt Elizabeth for several days. Every morning when I open the old cream suitcase to get clean clothes I breathe in its faint, sweet scent of Softasilk hand cream and Helena Rubinstein White Magnolia talc. It is the smell of my mother.

My brother and I are kindly looked after, and we are well fed. There is Weetbix with sugar for breakfast, and plenty of milk and cream because my uncle runs a dairy herd. Nicky and Anne are too young to be proper playmates, but my brother and I have each other, and it's the summer holidays.

We go to bed every evening before it's really dark. Usually there is enough daylight coming through the holland blind to allow me to read. I find unexplored treasures in a bookshelf in the bedroom, among them a book called *Josephine Goes Shopping*.[1] The illustrations show toys that have come to life and have adventures with the little girl who owns them. The book seems interestingly old-fashioned to me, and the watercolour illustrations in their pretty pastel shades exert a strong fascination. I would give anything in the world to be Josephine and have adventures with my toys: after my brother, my teddy bear is my best friend. My favourite Josephine character is Quacky Jack, a spindle-legged, orange-beaked toy duck who wears a sailor suit. Quacky Jack is a bit naughty, a bit of a rebel – something I admire, because I am not.

I read until the light fades and I can no longer make out the words.

Whose book is this? I suppose it belonged to either my aunt or my uncle, in the unimaginably distant past when they were young.

While I am a guest in this house, I see things I have previously ignored.

One of them is the framed black-and-white photograph of a man on the mantelpiece in the living room. He wears a dark uniform and a peaked cap, and above his coat pocket there are little wings. He looks quite a lot like my uncle, but I know my uncle only has one brother, Bruce, his identical twin. I ask my aunt who the man is, and she tells me that he is Uncle David's older brother, Glen. He was in the air force. He was killed in the war.

I have seen lots of framed photographs of men who were in the war, on shelves and sideboards and dressing-tables in other people's homes. We have three at home. Two of them are of my mother's younger brother. One shows him in an army slouch hat, and the other shows him as a naval officer with a white peaked cap and wiggly braid on his sleeves. (This means that he is an *officer*, my mother tells me.) The third photograph, and the biggest, is of my father. He is wearing a coat with the collar turned up, and an air force cap that looks like a triangle.

None of the people in these photographs has died. All of them are smiling. They look as if they are pleased to be photographed.

Glen died, though. I feel sad about it, even though he's only my uncle's brother, and that means he's not really related to me. I wonder how he died. Only old people are supposed to die.

The war has been over for as long as I have been alive, but that isn't very long. There are reminders of it everywhere. We live in Eden Valley, an area settled by German people, but we don't think of them as 'the Hun' or 'the Bosch', expressions I have heard men use.[2] They are just our neighbours. At school the children, even those with German names, think it's funny to use the insulting term 'Jerry'. I know that 'jerry' is also the slang name for a potty. (Q. Where can you find Jerry? A. Half full, under the bed.)

We have various objects at home that are souvenirs of the war, but 'war' isn't what you think of when you look at them. They are as anodyne as the little varnished Dutch wooden clog that my grandparents (Gran and Grandad Vigar, not the Melbourne ones) gave me when they returned from their world tour. These war souvenirs include a clock that used to be in the cockpit of an aeroplane, and three small blunt-nosed model Spitfires cast from old machine-gun bullet casings (my father told me this, so it is knowledge infused with great personal importance). Other less obvious mementoes linger. There are ration tickets for petrol and butter in the spotty box on the cedar sideboard, and my father's metal dog tags, strung on what looks like a knotted black bootlace, are in the sideboard drawer along with the round cork table-mats and the ivory-handled fish knives in a box lined with orange satin. The dog tags say that my father is C of E, but I'm sure this isn't true, because he never goes to church.

My mother's white VAD veil, with its important red cross, is in my dress-up drawer in the spare room.[3] And in the wall cupboard off the kitchen hangs a heavy fleece-lined leather flying jacket. I don't know where it came from. My father was in the air force, but he was a mechanic, not a pilot. Not an *officer*.

I know that my father volunteered for service almost as soon as war was declared. Little more than a year after his enlistment he was discharged as permanently unfit for duty. There was something wrong with his thyroid, my mother tells me. Her serious face suggests, rather thrillingly, that it was life-threatening.

I am proud of my father. Unlike other sturdier, less brave men who waited to be conscripted – biting their nails, hiding behind doors – he *wanted* to join up. He might not have served overseas, I think, and he might not have been an officer, but he is still a hero.

Uncle David's older brother, the man in the photograph, was in the air force, too, but his uniform is not like my father's. He wears a peaked cap with a crown on the front, and another pair of little wings.

After about a week our father collects us and drives us home again. Our mother is there already, waiting for us. She seems unchanged, but our father warns us that we must be quiet and on our best behaviour because she needs to get her strength back.

There is inexpressible comfort in knowing our mother is sleeping in the room across the hallway, and eating food that somehow tastes better because it has been prepared by her. At night I wait, dozing, until I can hear her rustling down the hallway, warm from her bath, in her shabby old slippers and her quilted blue satin dressing-gown.

Many years later, I discover (because I am now old enough to wonder about it, and to ask her) that my mother had suffered an ectopic pregnancy. Our father drove her all the way to hospital in Town, a trip that takes over an hour. By the time she arrived, she was close to death.

If we had not escaped this catastrophe, if the terrible blow had fallen, how different our lives would have been.

I am struck by the arbitrariness of it all.

What if she had died?

What if the baby had lived?

Either way, my life – all our lives – would have been different in so many ways. She didn't die, and the baby could never have survived, so all these possibilities are irrelevant. But what if?

Chapter 2

Avon Brae

Love for one's home is a strange thing. It's a feeling of possession, of belonging: of *right*.

Avon Brae, the Eden Valley property where my father and my brother and I were born, is stamped on every shred of my being. Even as a small child I felt a fierce, disparaging love for it, a love that both recognised and forgave all its many imperfections. A lifetime later, I know that I could close my eyes and recognise instantly its particular smell, a mixture of tobacco, linoleum polish and Palmolive soap, with undertones of ash and leather. I could hear the eager posse of mewling cats rushing to the back door, the harsh squeak of the door as it opens and the flat clunk of its closing. I could feel the warmed concrete of the courtyard beneath my bare feet, and the cool soft grass of the backyard patch of lawn.

Decades later my memory places me at the entrance to the driveway, and the old place leaps to life, as real as ever.

The uneven, slightly raised drive is shaded to the left by a line of ragged pine trees standing ankle deep in crunchy brown needles. In summer the air smells of pine resin and dust. On the other side of the pine trees is the horse paddock with its reefs of grey-green sandstone and its gnarled red gums. It hasn't held a horse in my lifetime, but small flocks of sheep wander, grazing. Beyond the wire fence to my right is an ancient orchard of twiggy plum trees splashed with yellow lichen. The fruit they bear is scanty, small and hard, barely worth the picking. Along the fence that forms a boundary with the road, bushy olive trees raise their silvery leaves in the wind like flocks of birds wheeling.

The drive itself is of dirty white gravel. Countless tyres passing on either side of the sparsely grassed middle strip have pounded the stony surface so that it's as firm as concrete. There are long shallow dips where milky water collects after rain. The pine trees create heavy shade, pierced by intermittent sunlight.

A few steps further on, the house is visible through the trees that surround it. I see flashes of the white-framed sunroom windows, a curved expanse of grey corrugated-iron roof.

Now at my left is the hedge, a high green wall marking domestic from rural land. Here the driveway turns in a smooth arc, passing the smaller of two rockeries, encircling the lawn with its narrow concrete border and the purple lilac bush. The lawn is of small-leafed lippia, hazardous to bare feet: buzzing bees hover over its tiny flowers. The driveway passes the front door, and then the side door, and mingles at last with the grass and bare earth outside the garages and the wheat shed, linking with the plain dirt driveway that has sidled around from the other side of the house.

The side door has always been our main door. A knock at the real front door indicates the arrival of a stranger. Friends use the side door. Others, like the Rawleigh's man who sells spices and soap, vanilla essence and hair oil, go directly to the back.

Avon Brae as I remember it

To the right of the door is the sleep-out, a narrow enclosure which takes up two thirds of the veranda. As well as the sleep-out, the veranda contains a garden bench, painted white, a heavy black cast-iron boot-scraper, and a thin, fraying coir doormat. Hanging on the stone wall is a nautical barometer, its case powdery with verdigris.

The already small space of the sleep-out is divided into two rooms by a thin wall of dimpled grey asbestos sheeting. My mother tells me that 'workmen or shearers' once slept there. The doors to each room are half flywire, with a spring-loaded closure. It must be bitterly cold in there on frosty nights, but I imagine that workmen are used to such conditions.

The main door is a double affair with two beautiful lead-light panels, deep purple irises with green leaves, made by Great-Aunt Charlotte Murray. I have only the vaguest idea who she is, but she is a relative of my father's and therefore of mine, and she is very good at working with stained glass. She is also good at collecting shells (a box of these, some of them chalk-white and spiky, with smooth, shiny apricot throats, is hidden somewhere in the chaos of the corrugated-iron garage).

I jump up the veranda steps – one, two – and open the door.

That dearly loved, rather dilapidated, largely inconvenient home now exists only in my memory. Nearly fifty years ago, in an act of bravado and desperation, my father, struggling financially, sold Avon Brae to a more prosperous neighbour. ('It's gone,' he said, coming back into the dining room after answering a knock on the back door. My mother took the news quite calmly.)

Years later the property was sold again, to complete strangers, city people. I saw photographs of it in the Real Estate section of the *Advertiser*. This time it went for hundreds of thousands of dollars. Eden Valley, once a sheep-farming and general farming district, had become newly desirable as a place where vineyards thrived. There is more money in wine than in wool.[1]

In the years since we left Avon Brae the house has been made over, modernised, prettified with cast-aluminium lace. It has been given slickness and gloss, polished wood floors, French windows and a swimming pool. Lawns mask and gentrify areas once filled by tin sheds and rusting car bodies, dog kennels and the chook yard. The outside lavatory standing sentinel beside the clothesline, and the clothesline itself, a square of sagging wires supported by wooden clothes props, have been swept away along with the cypress hedge, the rockeries, the orchards, the sleep-out and the sunroom. The night-thumping possums in the roof will certainly have been evicted, the streaks of their reddish urine scrubbed from the walls and painted over (although nothing ever quite gets rid of the smell).

A neat sign at the entrance to the driveway now announces the property's name. We never needed that: everybody knew who we were. *We* knew who we were.

My grandfather, William Thomas Vigar, had the house built by a local builder.[2] He designed it, shaped its bluestone walls, floored it with jarrah and roofed it with iron. Avon Brae was his marital home, and the home of the girls who became my aunts, and the boy who became my father. For a while it was also, although this is something I realised only recently, the home of my uncle's brother Glen, and indeed of my uncle too, and his twin. I didn't know this until my uncle told me, and suddenly it placed my home, my familiar home, in a new and unfamiliar light.

Avon Brae has been a part of all our lives.

There are, there must be, ghosts.

Chapter 3

2000 and Beyond

Decades have passed since 1967, the year our family was expunged from the life of a district where it had had a firm foothold since the mid-nineteenth century. It was 1856 when my great-grandfather, William Matthews Vigar, emigrated to South Australia to manage the 5,378-acre estate of his 'uncle Matthews'. Thomas Matthews had come to the Eden Valley district even earlier, in 1840.[1]

As we move inexorably towards the twenty-first century, my father has been dead for some years (in 1991, of prostate cancer, at the age of seventy-five), and my gentle, laughing Aunt Elizabeth has been diagnosed with Alzheimer's disease. At first none of us believes this diagnosis. She seems a little dreamy, a little distant, sometimes a little erratic. But not really *changed*. Not *ill*. My mother, who loves her sister-in-law dearly, is confident that the doctors have made a mistake. They do sometimes, she assures me, as we have afternoon tea together in the small Myrtle Bank unit where she now lives (Irish apple cake, from Pat-a-Cake down the road: my mother no longer bakes, and her cake tins lie rusting in the kitchen cupboard). But my aunt is in her late seventies now, so we admit that it is possible.

By the time that possibility has become a certainty, my mother is herself dead. She died in 2000, the year before the date of her birthday, 11 September, became known around the world as 9/11.

It is a long time since the Murries lived just three miles away from us down a country road. In 1961 Uncle David took up a position as an Agricultural Officer in the Department of Agriculture, Stock and Fisheries in Papua New Guinea. By then he and Elizabeth had four children: Nicholas, Anne, Jane and Andrew; baby Thomas, born in 1956, had died when he was only three months old. David was posted to Papua New Guinea in March 1961, and the rest of the family joined him in June. They stayed there for nearly nine years, and when they returned to South Australia they bought a home in the Adelaide suburb of Magill. Their lives were shattered in 1985 by the death of Andrew, their youngest son, in a car accident. Somehow they hauled themselves through their grief to recover some sort of normality.

After my aunt's diagnosis she and David sold the Magill house where they had lived for thirty years. They moved to a neat red brick unit in the War Veterans' Home in Myrtle Bank, a large lawned retirement complex that included a secure nursing home.

By 2003 my aunt's condition has worsened to the point where my uncle can no longer care for her, and she has become a resident in the nursing home. Her room has been made pleasant and comfortable. There are flowers, cushions, a mohair rug for her knees. Carefully placed photographs create instant memories of her wedding day (she is laughing, always laughing), of her children, of herself as a young Mothercraft nurse. Her children and her grandchildren visit her as often as they can. Her granddaughters, now in their early twenties, laugh and chatter and paint her nails and do her hair. She is now completely dependent, unable to walk, confined to her bed or a recliner chair. Her memory is dwindling to a pinprick of light in darkness, but still there are flashes of her old self. A ghost of her laughing smile sometimes illuminates her face as a tiny memory is retrieved and savoured. Who knows what she thinks, what she remembers as she disappears into the awful void of her illness?

I am not sure she knows who I am, but the sweetness of her fleeting smile makes me blink back sudden tears. She cannot say my name, in spite of my uncle's prompting.

My uncle cares for her with great tenderness. He sits beside her every day, talking to her, stroking her hand. His will be the last face she remembers.

In November 2006 my aunt and uncle move to Ardrossan, on Yorke Peninsula. There are two reasons for this: David's younger sister Gwenyth lives there, and the town has a good nursing home. It is here that Elizabeth dies, aged almost eighty-seven, in May 2008.

In October 2013 David, still living in Ardrossan, has turned ninety, and his family has organised a birthday party for him. The inevitable sad memories are forbidden because there are nine decades of a well-lived life to celebrate. Among those celebrating are his three remaining children, eleven grandchildren and several great-grandchildren. In them I see glimpses of my aunt's smile, echoes of her distinctive voice. Her daughters, Anne and Jane, have become in middle age increasingly like her.

This is the sort of family one is pleased to belong to. The genes are good: my uncle's ninety years sit on him gracefully, and his many descendants are tall, healthy, cheerful, free-spirited, friendly people. His twin, Bruce, can't be here, but he is alive and well on the Sunshine Coast, where he now lives. The brothers remain close.

Everybody has brought food for the party. Home-baked fruit cakes and iced sponges and buttered scones and egg sandwiches with shredded lettuce jostle plates of gourmet cheeses and pickled olives and small salty crackers. Cups and mugs are filled and re-filled with tea, sugar is spooned and stirred. Conversations are loud and exclamatory as relatives who haven't met since the most recent funeral re-connect, catch up, remind themselves of who they are. Country manners, country voices, blend with the accents of Adelaide's eastern suburbs; creaky old voices are drowned out by young laughter. Tweed sports coats and striped ties mingle with shorts and thongs and logo T-shirts, plaid flannelette shirts and the boots my father used to call 'laughing sides'. There are babies and toddlers, and at least one pregnant granddaughter. This family is durable. It will go on, and on.

I've known for some time now that I am related to my uncle by more than just his marriage to my father's sister. Although I've never investigated it properly, it seems that I also have some sort of blood tie to his side of the family. The relationship is distant, at best – a connection via the Murrays rather than the Murries. My father is descended from the Murrays: I know that much. But where does the Murray/Murrie link come in?

I speak to a cousin, who knows not much more than I do. 'I'm putting together a family history,' she says. 'I'll give you a call.'

On a sideboard I see, among the birthday cards (*90 today! Congratulations!*), a framed photograph of my father as a young man in his air force uniform. It's a photo I haven't seen before, and seeing it gives me a jolt. *Hello*, I think. *What are you doing here?* I know there's no reason why he shouldn't be there: after all, he is my aunt's older brother, and she was very fond of him. But seeing him like this, unexpectedly, and in an unfamiliar context, removes him from me. For just a second, before certainty kicked in, I saw him as a stranger.

Towards the end of the afternoon, as the crowd of guests begins to thin out, I go into another room to see my uncle's latest artworks. He is an accomplished copyist who, as a hobby, uses photographs of people and places as the basis for oil paintings. There on the wall is a lovingly rendered painting of my aunt; there are various family homesteads, including my own (which is no longer my own); there is the adored son who died on a country road more than a quarter of a century ago.

But my eye is caught by a framed black-and-white photograph of a young man in the peaked cap of an RAAF officer.

He smiles confidently from behind the glass, and I feel the same odd shock of surprise and connection I felt when I saw the photograph of my father. Both of them young men, both in the air force. One lived, the other died.

I stare at that handsome, impossibly youthful face, and the years fall away, and I am a child again, back in the living room at Ravenswood, and my aunt is telling me who the man is. He's Glen, the older brother. The third brother.

Glen is part of our family, I think, and yet I know nothing about him except that he died in the war. There must be more to his story, a great deal more. Suddenly I want to know what it is.

Chapter 4

Families

A family is like a pack of cards. There are the picture cards, the kings and queens and jacks, colourful and known and familiar. They are the established ones, secure in their historical places: grandparents, fathers and mothers, brothers and sisters. There is the occasional black sheep in the form of a Joker. Then, moving down the scale, there are all the others: cousins known and unknown, babies (a two of clubs, a three of hearts); great-aunts and great-uncles, second and third cousins, relatives removed and not removed. Most of these are fairly low value cards, but the pack is not complete without them. At the head of all these card people are the aces, the important ones from whom all this scattering of red and black minor cards has descended.

I'll start with the Murrays.

Hanging on the wall of my present home is a painting, on a thin wooden panel, of one of the rural properties once owned by my family: Glen Turret, near Truro, founded by my great-great-grandfather, Pulteney Malcolm Murray.[1]

Pulteney Malcolm Murray, a Scottish sheep-farmer and sheep-breeder from Langholm, Dumfries, was born in 1817 and came to South Australia in 1839. He is very much an ace card. Twice married, he fathered (I think – the records are not completely reliable) twenty-one children, of whom fourteen survived to adulthood. His descendants today would be numbered in the hundreds.

The Glen Turret painting is the work of an artist revealed only by his initials in the corner, preceding the date, which is 1875. The letters are difficult to read, but tentatively I make them out to be G.E.B.H. The final letter is particularly obscure, and might be a K, or an R. My father once told me that the artist was a Frenchman who travelled the country, taking commissions to paint properties as he went. My father was given to making this sort of untested assertion, and I have no way of knowing if this one is true or not. It is in effect a portrait of the property as it was at the time of painting: a record rather than a work of art. In later years a photograph would have done the same thing, more accurately, less charmingly.

The painting shows the property in springtime, shearing time. The holding pens of the shearing shed to the left of the homestead are chock-a-block with sheep. Hints of yellow flowers are daubed into the bright green grass, and the orchard trees in front of the house are stippled with pink and white blossom.

This painting has been in our possession ever since I can remember. Before I had it restored, it was dulled with a patina of dirty varnish. The dark veneer on the wooden frame had broken and peeled off here and there, exposing naked pine, and the gilt inner frame was spotted with tarnish. The wooden panel was slightly warped, its hanging wire tangled. A deep scratch disfigured the sky, a permanent lightning bolt ripping across a pale yellowish cloud through which the grain of the wood was visible.

The painting itself is, to be honest, variable. Although

some of the work is of high quality – the exquisite rendering of the square stone homestead itself, and the shearing shed, with each penned sheep shown in careful detail, and dray-loads of wool bales being hauled away by draught-horses – the foreground is spoiled by three cows. Two of them look perfectly cow-like, but the one lying down in the centre foreground has been clumsily rendered, with an awkwardly protruding rump, a too-small head and a foolish expression.

The 1875 painting of Glen Turret, with That Cow in the foreground

Largely because of this implausible cow, my mother refused to hang the painting anywhere in the house. When we lived at Avon Brae it was stored in what was always called 'the maid's room', along with other unwanted things that were nevertheless too significant to throw out: old army ammunition boxes, a tin naval dress trunk, assorted crockery, bundled editions of *Punch* and the *Bulletin* and the *Illustrated London News*.

With the print-out of a family tree in my hand I look at the painting now, trying to make sense of what, and who, it shows.[2]

To one side of the homestead four tiny painted doll-like figures stand in a line beside a grove of trees. They have pinpoint eyes but no mouths or noses. Beneath the trees white geese are grazing; nearer to the house, it's possible to make out a peacock (tail down) and a peahen. The tallest of the four human figures, a girl or woman wearing a red dress, holds a baby in long white clothes. The other three, judging from their size, are young children, two girls and a boy. Other people, less well defined, are also in the picture. A woman in a black dress with a bustle drifts past the side of the house, approaching the figure of a male person (her husband?) a short distance away. I realise with a small shock of excitement that she is my great-great-grandmother, Elizabeth Murray, who would then have been only thirty-seven years old and was already (good grief) the mother of ten children. In front of the house two boys of similar size appear to be playing some sort of slingshot ball game, standing on either side of a small tree and watched by (I try to make it out from the scanty brushstrokes) what might be either a small kangaroo or a younger child. Another male figure, possibly the oldest boy, is positioned closer to the shearing shed.

In 1875 there should be nine children in the family, and

the painting shows only eight. I know that one daughter, also named Elizabeth, died in 1871 at the age of eleven. Perhaps another child died too, or perhaps the artist accidentally left him, or her, out of the painting. Two more babies were born after 1875: a girl, who lived for only a year, and a boy.

Referring again to the family tree, I try to identify the children. My great-grandmother Mary Ann was born in 1859. She was the oldest daughter, so it's likely that she is the tallest child in the row of four, the one holding the baby. In 1875 she would have been fifteen or sixteen, still not old enough to put up her hair and let down her skirts. She and the two smaller girls wear white bonnets and mid-length frocks, while the boy is distinguished by his black clothes and his round black hat. The smallest bonneted girl is probably two-year-old Charlotte, who became Great-Aunt Charlotte, the artist in stained glass and collector of shells. Another tiny mystery solved. That being the case, the other little girl is either Esther (seven) or Effie (four). The boy can only be William (six). The baby is clearly Arthur, who was born in 1874. In the family pack of cards he has two pips, no more.

By a process of elimination, I decide that one of the boys with the supposed kangaroo is Ernest, Pulteney and Elizabeth's fourth child. He would have been eleven in 1875 – just the right sort of age to play boisterous ball games and have a bush animal for a pet. His brother Francis, just a year younger, must be the boy on the other side of the tree.

I pore over the painting, trying to bring the figures to life. Clearly the artist has reproduced, as faithfully as he can, both what he sees in front of him and what his client has asked him to paint. If it exists in the painting, whether it's a horse or a peacock or a baby, then it existed in real life. With extraordinary vividness G.E.B.H., whoever he is, has depicted the life of this past generation of family, these people whose bloodlines I share.

An old photograph, greyish, a little blurry, dated 1916 or 1917, brings some of the main cards in the pack more clearly into focus. It shows four generations of women in my family. There she is in real life, the distant black-clad woman in my painting: my great-great-grandmother, Elizabeth Murray (*née* Vigar), several decades older. Her wispy white hair is pulled back from her wise old face, and she wears a capacious cotton print dress of the sort worn by country women

The four generations. From left: Elizabeth Murray (*née* Vigar), Emily Vigar (*née* Shannon), Mary Ann Shannon (*née* Murray), and (in front) little Kathleen Vigar (later Murray)

in the mid-nineteenth century. Twelve times a mother, she seems almost insubstantial next to her more amply proportioned daughter Mary Ann Shannon (*née* Murray), my great-grandmother, who is stylish in a fitted costume with covered buttons. I imagine the colour of the costume to be something like Prussian blue, but it may well be a fashionable heliotrope, or a more sober brown. It's wartime, and at least one of her sons is overseas, serving in Egypt with the Ninth Light Horse, so perhaps gaiety of clothing isn't appropriate. Both these women are long widowed: between them, astonishingly, they had *at least* twenty-three children. ('Some died in infancy', the Shannon family history book says in a casual sort of way.)[3]

Standing behind these two women is Mary Ann's daughter, my own grandmother, Emily Vigar (*née* Shannon). She is sister to the Light Horse soldier, who is Len Shannon: presumably he was a favourite brother, because my father was named after him. In the photograph she is wearing a plain cotton blouse and a dark skirt with a belt. Although she is in her mid-thirties here, she looks about the same age as her own mother. I don't believe my grandmother ever looked young. Searching back in my mind, I remember her withered but still imposing face, her forthright pale-blue gaze. 'Come and give your old gran a kiss,' she'd say, whenever she visited, and my brother and I would hang back shyly before darting forward to deliver the required endearment. Gran's hair was wispy, too, like her grandmother's, and she was always pushing errant floating strands behind her ears. I remember seeing her, when I was very young, getting ready for bed, the grey-white bun surprisingly transformed into a thin braid that fell down her back. She died, in care, diabetic and almost blind, when I was at university. I wish I had known her better – what stories she could have told! It is a loss that can never be made up.

Sitting in a child's wicker chair in front of the three matriarchs from whom she is descended is Gran's older daughter Kathleen, aged about three, holding a small doll. She was a pretty child, and she became an even prettier woman who married into another branch of the Murray clan and became herself the matriarch of a large, wealthy, successful landed family. Here she wears buttoned boots, and her hair has been done in shining sausage ringlets. A wickerwork pram for the doll is nearby. My father, who would at this time have been a young baby, does not make an appearance. As a boy, he is irrelevant to this historical photograph of four generations of women. My younger aunt, Elizabeth, would not be born for another four or five years. The only other living thing in the photograph is, unexpectedly, a white cockatoo on a perch.

The photograph fascinates me. I have inherited some of the genetic characteristics of these three women, and so have my children. We are cut from the same cloth. My daughter has the same fine, silky hair as my grandmother. I have my great-great-grandmother's small head. What else do our common genes contain? Myopia, cancer, chalky teeth, a sense of humour, a talent for music or cooking or art? Our first and middle names – Emily, Anne, Elizabeth, Mary – are carried on down the generations.

I investigate the family tree again. It is a dense-looking document, its vertical and horizontal lines revealing myriad intermarriages of the main branches of the family, going back for generations. They crop up again and again, in different permutations: the Murrays, the Murries, the Inglises, the Logans, the Shannons, the Vigars. At the head of each branch is the date of immigration and the name of the sailing ship that brought these determined and hopeful immigrants from Scotland, Ireland and England to South Australia. They arrived at Port Adelaide on the *Fairfield* and the *Lady Lillford* in 1839, on the *John Pirie* in 1843, on the *Ramillies* and the *David Malcolm* in 1849, on the *Dirigo* and the *Northern Light* in 1854, on the *Switzerland* in 1856. Some came as single men and women, others as families.[4]

The families are invariably large, with broods of eight, ten, twelve children. It's not uncommon for brothers and sisters from one family to marry sisters and brothers from another, becoming their own in-laws. Nephews and nieces are also first or second cousins. Although there's not the smallest taint of in-breeding, the family tree is as complicated as a Fair Isle knitting pattern.

At the joint head of the Murray family tree is my great-great-grandmother Elizabeth. Her story now seems to me quite astonishing, although at the time it may not have been unusual. Elizabeth Vigar was born in Moorlinch, Somerset, in 1838, and sailed to South Australia aboard the *David Malcolm*, alone, when she was just ten years old. (Children under fourteen were allowed to make the voyage for a reduced cost, just £1, and I expect that her parents, who were thrifty, hard-working farmers, took this into consideration.) She would never see her Somerset home or her parents again.

Elizabeth arrived in South Australia on 7 April 1849 and joined her thirteen-year-old brother, Joseph, who had arrived two weeks earlier, and another older brother,

Edward. At some stage she lived in the settlement then known as Rhine Villa, and since renamed Cambrai. She may have worked as a servant there. Edward had already settled in the Truro area, and probably kept an eye on his younger siblings. They may even have made their home with him, helping him to establish a farm of his own.

On 10 February 1857 Elizabeth Vigar married the considerably older Pulteney Malcolm Murray. He was at this time a widower with four children surviving of the nine born to his first wife, *née* Mary Ann Scott, who had died just three months earlier. His new bride was eighteen and already pregnant. I don't know how Pulteney and Elizabeth met: it may be that she was a servant in his household, or a nursemaid to his young children. Was it a love match, or simply a matter of sense and expediency? Photographs reveal that Pulteney, a balding, bushy-bearded man with pale, prominent eyes, was not at all handsome, and he was more than twice Elizabeth's age. He was, however, intelligent, ambitious and relatively prosperous, and his property, Glen Turret, was a substantial one. By almost any measure the marriage was both successful and highly productive.

Elizabeth Murray bore children at regular intervals until 1879, when her husband died, possibly from tuberculosis, at the age of sixty-two. She was only forty-one when she became a widow. She lived on to the then remarkable age of eighty-seven, and at some point early in the 1920s the young girl who had made the long voyage from England to Australia on her own became the oldest woman in Australia ever to go on an aeroplane flight. A photograph shows her standing with companions next to a bi-plane, her thin frame enveloped in a long duster coat, a close-fitting leather flying helmet making her small head look even smaller.[5] She died in 1925. Her oldest daughter, Mary Ann Shannon (*née* Murray), my great-grandmother, survived her by only four years.

The more I look at the family tree, the more it begins to make sense. Some things now become apparent to me.

One. My great-grandmother Mary Ann Shannon's brother Ernest Murray (the second son of Elizabeth and Pulteney, and possibly one of the small boys playing the slingshot game in my Glen Turret painting) was my uncle David Murrie's grandfather. Ernest's third daughter, Lulu Murray, married George Murrie and gave birth to three boys and a girl. (The Murray/Murrie connection!) The girl was Gwenyth, and the three boys were my uncle, his twin Bruce, and Glen.

Two. This means that Mary Ann Shannon's daughter, my grandmother Emily Vigar (*née* Shannon), was Lulu Murrie's first cousin. As a result . . .

Three. My uncle and I are indeed related by more than his marriage to my father's sister Elizabeth. We are also, in fact, second cousins, once removed.

Four. This means, obviously, that I have the same relationship to Glen, the man in the photograph. We too are kin.

It's like seeing my father surrounded by birthday cards, in a place where he doesn't seem to belong; and yet he does belong there. It's just that I didn't realise it.

Pulteney Malcolm Murray and Elizabeth Murray are Glen Murrie's great-grandparents, and my great-great-grandparents. It's as simple as that.

In an instant, a three of hearts has become a picture card.

‘What are you writing now?’ my son asks. He lives in Canada, and we Skype most weekends.

I tell him what I’m writing. I tell him that my uncle had an older brother who was killed in the war, and I’m trying to find out more about him. Briefly I recount the details of his life.

‘It sounds like a short story to me,’ my son says. He has a way of coming to the point.

‘It’s a lot more than that,’ I say. ‘But actually there isn’t any story.’

My son looks sceptical. He’s a scientist, after all. ‘So how are you going to write it?’ he asks.

How indeed?

The Canadian writer Margaret Atwood once spoke of our belief that the dead don’t own their history. This, she says, gives us permission to write about them, to use their lives for our own purposes. But should it?

What gives me the right to tell the story of a man I never knew? Am I drawing dishonestly on the family connection?

I am not sure I can answer these questions.

How do you conjure up a person you have never met? How do you reconstruct, in words, a body from which the last breath was ripped seven decades ago? Illuminate an inner life long gone, a life brimming with fears and emotions and dreams? It seems impertinent even to try. Why should I think I am even remotely equal to such a task?

I know only the barest facts about him. His name was Glen Inglis Murrie. He was born, he grew up, he died. It is his death, and particularly the manner of his dying, that singles him out. Yes, he is family, but that’s a tenuous connection. There are many others more closely related to him than I am: brothers and a sister, nieces and nephews, great-nieces and great-nephews, all of them now older than he was when his life was snuffed out.

I imagine him at his brother David's ninetieth birthday party, still youthful, seeing his siblings in old age, struggling to place his relatives, almost all of them born after the war. The family has continued to grow and multiply, leaving him behind. He is frozen in time, a black-and-white image in pilot's uniform, forever young.

I start to write about Glen. Or rather, I begin to accumulate information about him, about his family. Collecting details becomes an obsession. In my mind these details will cohere in a colourful tapestry from which he will emerge, fully rounded and alive. All I have to do is construct a skeleton of facts and imagine the rest.

There isn't a story, though, I argue. (I argue with myself quite a lot.) How can you tell a story when there isn't one? There are no mysteries to be solved. No murders, no incest, no legal tangles. No drugs are involved. No illicit sex, no infidelity, no child abuse, no kidnappings, no family feuds. What is a story without one of these to keep the reader involved and wanting to know more?

I phone my uncle and ask him what Glen was like. How does he remember him?

'He was a good person,' my uncle replies.

'But what was he *really* like?' I say. 'What *sort* of person was he? What do you remember most about him?'

There is a brief silence. Then, 'Well . . . he was just an excellent character,' says my uncle's deep voice. 'An excellent character.'

Chapter 5

Searching

The date today, as I write, is 23 September 2014. It is exactly seventy years since Glen died.

So.

First of all, what can I find out about his background – his parents and grandparents? I already know quite a lot about the Murray side of his family, but what about the Murries?

Armed with clues provided by my uncle, I begin to explore.[1]

I find out that Glen's father, George Inglis Murrie, was born in 1894 and spent his boyhood in the mid-north town of Georgetown. The third of four sons, he was descended from two prominent rural families. His paternal grandfather, Peter Murrie, and his maternal grandfather, George Inglis, were both Scottish. Both had arrived in South Australia in 1854, George as a seventeen-year-old with his family on the *Dirigo*, and Peter, aged twenty-three, on the *Northern Light*. Before long both men were married (Peter to Mary Currie, and George to Eliza Scott Davidson) and had begun to raise large families of their own. Both men had a long association with Georgetown. Both became JPs.

George Inglis farmed in various parts of South Australia before he took up land near Georgetown in 1869. Here, as stated in his comprehensive obituary, he 'took a leading part in all movement for the welfare of the town and the neighbourhood'.[2] His home, Springfield, was 'celebrated for its happy hospitality and for the genial kindness of the host and hostess'. George was the first chairman of the Georgetown District Council, the founder and first president of the Georgetown Institute, and a trustee of the Clover Hill Baptist Church. He was a frequent delegate to interstate conferences on the scourge of rust in wheat, where 'the value of his services was freely admitted as those of a well known practical farmer'. In 1886 he was appointed to the Board of Trustees of the State Bank, and from 1900 he was its chairman. By this time he had moved to Knightsbridge, a moderately well-to-do and thoroughly respectable suburb in eastern Adelaide. (Its name no longer exists, because in 1941 it was taken over by the joint suburbs of Leabrook and Hazelwood Park.)

George Inglis and his wife Eliza (of whom more later) had twelve children. Their oldest daughter, who was known as Sissy although her real name was Mary, was our George's mother and later, of course, the grandmother of Glen, David, Bruce and Gwenyth.

Sissy Inglis married Peter Murrie, who had been named after his father, in September 1884. When Peter sailed away with the 6th (South Australian Imperial Bushmen) Contingent to fight in the Boer War, he left a family of four sons: Alan, Bob, George and Thomas. The troops departed for South Africa on 6 April 1901. Little more than two months later, on 9 June, Sergeant Peter Murrie was dead of enteric fever at the age of thirty-nine. He is buried at Standerton in South Africa. ('Great sympathy is felt for his widow,' wrote a reporter for the *Advertiser*.)[3] The oldest of his sons, Alan, was sixteen. George was just seven.

Four years later the Murries were struck by another tragedy, a railway accident at Georgetown on 4 October 1905. This time the victim was George himself, now eleven years old. A report in the *Adelaide Chronicle* provides the horrific details:[4]

Some men were shunting trucks in the station-yard when the lad came into the station-yard, and, boylike, thinking he would be of some help got between the trucks, and was pulling on the coupling. He was not seen by the men. When he was crossing the points his boot caught between the rails. The boot burst, and the boy extricated himself, and tried to throw himself between the trucks; but the other leg got under the opposite wheels and the flesh was torn off the limb from the ankle to the hip. The men were startled by hearing screams, and the trucks were instantly stopped and pushed off the boy. He was carried home, and Dr. Chancellor was sent for. Dr. Chancellor ordered his removal to the Jamestown Hospital. The wound is a very ugly one, and is 2 ft. 4 in. long.

The wound became rotten with gangrene, and young George, his fear and distress unimaginable, was taken to another hospital. Here his leg was amputated just below the hip.

At some point after this, George and his widowed mother, Sissy, and his three brothers made the move to Knightsbridge, which was already the home of Sissy's parents, George and Eliza Inglis.

Born in 1840 at The Hermitage, near Houghton, Eliza Inglis, *née* Davidson, was celebrated as 'the first white girl' born in the Houghton district. She lived to the then unusual age of ninety, and on 27 March 1930 she was rewarded by an admiring birthday notice in the *News*:

She writes her own letters, waters the garden, rises at 7 o'clock in the morning, and rarely misses weekly worship at Knightsbridge Baptist Church . . . A daughter of Mr. and Mrs. T. Davidson, she was carried for 14 miles through scrub country as an infant, when her mother walked to Adelaide for her christening.

Eliza was locally famous – famous enough to be given the honour, at eighteen, of opening the newly completed road cutting at Tea Tree Gully, 'the longest in the state', in 1858.

There is no pictorial record of this event, or none that I can find, but I imagine her, dressed in virginal white and a flowered bonnet, looking a bit like a young Queen Victoria, cutting a ribbon. Seventeen years a widow, she died in 1931 at the age of ninety years and six months. Four of her twelve children, but not Sissy, predeceased her. At the time of her death she had thirty-five grandchildren and twenty-one great-grandchildren.[5]

Being widowed early runs in both sides of this family, the Murries and the Murrays. It's mostly the women who grow old. They don't seem to become ill: they just go on until they wear out, until they are tired from all the hard work of living.

The family of Lulu, Glen's mother, is a case in point.

Lulu was born and raised in Snowtown, roughly an hour's drive south of Georgetown. She was the third of four daughters born to Emily Mary Alice Murray, *née* Logan, and her husband Ernest. Emily Murray was generally known as Em.

Ernest Murray managed a sheep property, Hummocks Station, for members of Adelaide's aristocracy, the Barr Smith family. He died in 1905 at the early age of forty-one, leaving behind a family of strong, remarkable women. Emily Mary (Em) Murray died in 1961 at the age of ninety-three, having been a widow for fifty-six years. Her daughters, Joyce, Merle, Lulu and Gwenyth, made it to eighty-nine, ninety-four, ninety-nine, and ninety-eight, respectively. There was a son, too, the last child, but little Marcus Ernest died at eleven weeks, of whooping cough. Ernest is buried with his baby son at Snowtown.

While they lived in the country Lulu and her three sisters were educated by their mother, but after the death of her husband, Em Murray moved her family to Adelaide, to Knightsbridge. Lulu was eight years old when she went to school for the first time, attending Marryatville Primary School with her sisters.[6] Like the Murries and the Inglises, the Murrays became members of the Knightsbridge Baptist Church.

It is likely that Sissy Murrie (born in 1864) and Em Murray (born in 1868) saw each other as soulmates. Both had rural backgrounds, both were of Scottish descent, both were widowed early. Neither, apparently, had any thought of remarrying (women didn't then, as a rule, although widowed men, especially those with large numbers of children, quickly sought new partners and helpmates). Sissy had four sons, and Em had four daughters. They had a great deal in common.

As the entity that brought these two families together, the Knightsbridge church deserves a couple of paragraphs to itself. It was opened in 1884, and unlike many churches which have been turned into restaurants, beauty salons or nightclubs, it still functions as a place of worship. Square and solid, it is built of bluestone and given landmark status by an unusual porch featuring Spanish-inspired arches. The interior is spacious, plain and sensible, with two aisles and three ranks of pews, sufficient to accommodate a sizeable congregation. Words like 'meaningful' and 'dynamic' and 'ministry' feature on its website, and its 'welcome' text is also available in Korean and Chinese. All sections of the community are catered for, with regular meetings of specifically targeted groups (Craft, Friendship, Young Adults, Young Mums). Sermons are posted online. This is a serious church, a church as a business, a church determined to stay upbeat and relevant.

In the first decades of the twentieth century the ethnic mix on which the Knightsbridge Baptist Church now prides itself was very different. Non-British people were a rarity, and families attended church regularly as a matter of course.

It was through church attendance, and church activities, that Em Murray's third daughter Lulu and Sissy Murrie's third son George became better acquainted. Before long they began a courtship, going for walks, taking the tram to the beach, and occasionally going to the pictures. During her long engagement Lulu (who had completed a commercial course at high school and gone on to business college) collected items for her glory box and worked in the city, in a land agent's office. She and George married in 1920. In the same year George built a house at 15 Davenport Terrace,

Hazelwood Park, taking out a forty-year mortgage. It was a six-room brick house with an iron roof, and the young couple gave it the name Wandeen, an Aboriginal word meaning 'home' or 'camping place'.

George didn't allow himself to be held back because he had only one leg: the word 'disabled' simply didn't exist in his vocabulary. It didn't stop him from having a secure job as an accountant with the State Bank, or from heartily enjoying sporting activities. At one stage a prosthetic leg was created for him, but it was so heavy and cumbersome that after wearing it once he abandoned it, preferring his familiar single crutch. (In my mind's eye I see it: old-fashioned, wooden, with a rubber tip and a leather pad to fit into the armpit.) Using this crutch, George was both nimble and resourceful. He was the star of the bank's ping-pong team, and with his strong upper body and long arms he played a good game of tennis. He had a powerful serve (says his daughter Gwenyth, who remembers) and was almost unbeatable at the net.

George was a good and responsible father and husband. As was usual in those days, the roles of husband and wife were clearly defined, with the husband looking after the business side of things and the woman in charge of housekeeping and caring for the family. Children, Lulu observed, should 'look to their mother for gentleness and kindness and fairness'.[7]

Between them George and Lulu had in abundance all the proper qualities for a successful marital team: good sense and sober expectations combined with affection and respect.

Grandmother Murrie and Grandmother Murray played

a large part in their grandchildren's lives. They were a formidable pair. They had raised their own children and kept their families together virtually single-handed. They made difficult decisions, kept their households running, provided security in the absence of male partners, instilled proper values.

These women, and their daughters and granddaughters, were strong, sensible, capable and kind-hearted. They were consummate home-makers, dutiful church-goers, kindly but strict guardians of their children, caring members of their communities. Any one of them could, if required, chop firewood, milk a cow, make a bread poultice or a good beef tea, devise a sling for a sprained wrist, or nurse a child through anything from croup to measles. They were women (like my grandmother Emily Vigar) with definite opinions (negative) about socialism, the Labor Party and trade unions. They were makers of pickles, jams and preserves, bakers of scones and biscuits, knitters of socks and jumpers. Like their Scottish ancestors, they were careful with money. They bought only such items of ready-made clothing as were absolutely necessary: everything else was made by hand, using hard-wearing fabrics like calico and flannel. Shoes were repaired at home.

Family was everything to them. Their children were loved, but they were never indulged, and they were expected to do their share to keep the household running smoothly. From a very young age they were obedient, courteous and well behaved. They knew that the world was run by grown-ups. When they were grown up, it would be their turn.

Chapter 6

Wandeen

Glen Inglis Murrie, Lulu and George's first baby, was born at home, as was then usual, on 7 March 1922. Lulu was attended by a doctor and a nurse, and the nurse stayed for two weeks to help the young mother. Twenty months later, on 18 October 1923, the twins arrived, once again at home, once again with medical help. (Gwenyth, the youngest child, was the only one to be born in a hospital.) Lulu received a maternity benefit of £5 for Glen, and the same amount for David and Bruce, who apparently were seen by the Government as one birth and not as two separate babies.[1]

Coping with three boys under the age of two might sound like a daunting task, but Lulu loved babies, and she had plenty of experience in child-rearing. She had sometimes minded children after school, and before her marriage she had helped my grandmother look after my father. A sickly, colicky baby, born with a twisted intestine, little Lennie Vigar required dedicated care. The earliest photo I have of him shows a rather bug-eyed infant resting fatly against a brocade cushion. (In the early years of the twentieth century a plump child was a healthy child, so his tubbiness would have been considered a good thing.) My father had great affection for Lulu all his life, and always saw her more or less as a second mother.

Uncle David has given me photos of the little Murries. With their dark eyes and smooth, chubby faces they are strikingly beautiful children.

Glen, just fifteen months old

Item 1. Here is Glen, fifteen months old, in a pale embroidered romper suit and pompom slippers buttoned over short white socks. He is standing confidently on a fur rug, straight-legged. His hair still has baby curls at the back.

Item 2. Here are the three brothers, Bruce, David and Glen, hair brushed, posing for the camera. The twins, in cotton smocks, are almost indistinguishable from each other (as they will remain throughout their lives). Their older brother, only a little bigger, wears a hand-knitted jumper, befitting his seniority.

Item 3. And here they are again, slightly older, the twins smartly dressed in sailor suits, Glen in what appears to be a school blazer and a tie. Endearingly, his ears stick out. All three boys direct their gaze forward: the photographer may be holding up a toy or clicking his fingers to attract their attention. Glen is about five, no more; the twins look to be about three.

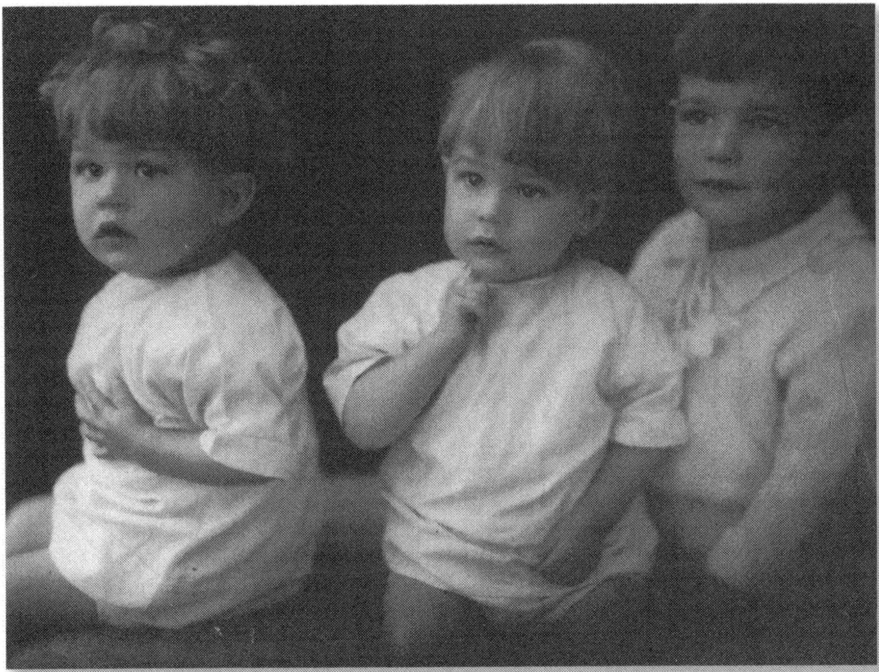

The three babies, Bruce, David and Glen, in about 1924

Glen, Bruce and David. The twins are perhaps three here, and Glen is four or five

Item 4. This one is a family snapshot, not formally posed. It shows the three brothers, barefoot, sitting at a child-sized table which bears a toy train and a toy tea-set. Glen sits in front of the tea-set. He looks down and away, as if thinking, and one foot half covers the other in a way that seems vaguely protective. The twins stare boldly at the camera. By this stage they have become a force to be reckoned with. My uncle tells me that they always shared the close-knit self-sufficiency peculiar to twins: kindred spirits, a team of two, needing no other members. In spite of his greater age, Glen may have felt subtly or even explicitly excluded. Three can be an awkward number, and to some degree the twins' solidarity may have constituted an automatic lock-out.

If he did feel a degree of solitariness, then the arrival of a baby sister on 29 March 1929 provided him with a welcome ally. Although Gwenyth was seven years younger than Glen, there was a special connection between them. He was always, she said, 'very kind' to her, and didn't tease her as the twins sometimes did. But in this snapshot she is yet to be born, and there are still just the three boys: the energetic, wriggly pair, stilled for ever by the release of the camera's shutter, and their pensive older brother.

The children's lives were happy and uneventful. Their home was not especially large or grand, but it was comfortable, with a wood stove in the kitchen, a chip heater in the bathroom and a wood-fired copper in the laundry. The kitchen had no hot water but it did have a cool safe, and later an icebox. The sitting room and dining room were warmed by open fireplaces. As in many country homes, most meals were eaten in the kitchen, but the dining room was the focus of family life. It was here, in the evenings, that

In the backyard at Wandeen

the children read (often, Lulu tells us, the encyclopaedia), or did their homework, or practised their music. The sitting room was reserved mainly for entertaining. There was a sleep-out as well as the three bedrooms, but the boys all shared a room. Country visitors were put up in a bedroom kept 'spare' for that purpose.

The house stood on a corner block, and had a picket fence down one side and a neatly trimmed hedge on the other. There were two fat palm trees in the front garden, and a rockery. The backyard had fruit trees and vegetables and a chookhouse. Feeding the chooks, collecting the eggs, and chopping kindling wood were regular chores shared by the boys as they grew older.

Food was good and plentiful. Groceries were delivered, and the milkman called twice a day. On the quiet suburban streets of Hazelwood Park the sound of a delivery man approaching in a horse-drawn van, stopping regularly, was a familiar one. The greengrocer, the butcher, the baker and the ice man all made regular rounds. Sometimes a fish man came round on his bicycle, or a rabbit-oh man. Orchardists from the nearby Adelaide Hills brought wooden cases of fruit for sale.

Following long-standing family tradition, the Murrie children were raised as Baptists. A strict code of behaviour was encouraged, and expected. In George and Lulu's home the children were not allowed to play noisy games on a Sunday, or ride their bikes, or play organised sport. Instead, they were encouraged to read quietly. A Sunday routine was scrupulously followed: Endeavour Society at ten o'clock, followed by the church service at eleven, and then Sunday School (at two o'clock) after lunch. Did the children sigh, I wonder, as Sunday with its restrictions dawned? Did they envy other children with greater freedom? The boys did play occasional pranks: Lulu recalls them letting off stink bombs, and at least one of them climbing a tree for an illicit smoke. The usual punishment for childish naughtiness was a period of confinement in the bathroom. Greater misdeeds might incur a smack, 'from Dad, usually'.

Entertainments, or at least those that cost money, were rare. Occasionally the children were taken to the pictures, to a matinee, but only if something special was showing. There was no lack of social activity, though, with church socials and fetes, school concerts and Sunday sing-alongs around the piano. Sometimes the whole family would take the train to Belair in the Adelaide Hills for a picnic. Every year they went to the Royal Show in Wayville, meeting country friends and relatives there.

Electric trams down Kensington Road provided regular access to Town. Like many others, the Murries travelled mainly by public transport. They didn't own a car until 1937, when George bought a second-hand Essex.

Life in the 1920s had an ease to it, a sunny predictability. The Great Depression was yet to hit. Men had jobs, and women had 'home duties'. Now that the First World War was over, the feeling of relaxation, of enjoying good times after so much hardship, must have been almost palpable. If men who survived the hell of the trenches had staring eyes and twitching faces, if they still suffered from panic attacks and nightmares and hallucinations, it was something to be hushed up. If Daddy was angry all the time, or if cheerful Uncle Bill now drank too much, it certainly wasn't discussed in front of children. The signs of physical wounds were common: men with scars, men with missing arms or legs, men with lungs ruined by the gas. Sometimes you might see an old soldier begging in the street. But few talked about the war, the horror of it, and especially not the returned men.

Reticence was part of maintaining the accepted boundaries. One didn't make a fuss: one just got on with things. To do otherwise indicated weakness. Stoicism was a virtue; so was manliness. The public or even private admission of fears or emotions wasn't considered manly. Counselling, the universal panacea today, hardly existed.

Perversely, and by way of deliberately ignoring the obvious, there was also an accepted sense that war, honourable war in defence of the nation, was something glorious. It brought out the best in people, turned ordinary men into heroes. An essential outing for the Murries, as for thousands of others, was the annual trip to Town to watch the soldiers march on Anzac Day, which by 1927 had become a public holiday Australia-wide.

Most people who lived in Adelaide's eastern suburbs were what was called 'middle class'. A few were 'upper class'. You could pick them because they lived in large old established houses, the sort that had leadlight and turrets, English trees in parklike grounds, a circular gravel driveway, a tennis court. The sons of the 'upper class' wore the school uniforms of one of the establishment schools, Saint's or Prince's or Scotch. Their daughters went to Presbyterian Girls' College, founded in 1922, or Walford, or Woodlands, or The Wilderness.

The Murries didn't aspire to be upper class. They were entirely content with who they were: a large extended middle-class family, honourable to a fault, staunchly loyal to each other, and more than happy with what life had seen fit to give them.

I imagine the family at their Hazelwood Park home, on a typical Saturday summer afternoon in about 1930. Glen is aged eight, David and Bruce are seven, Gwenyth is still a baby. The boys are playing cricket in the backyard while George listens to the final overs of a Sheffield Shield match on the wireless. (New South Wales is thumping South Australia at the Adelaide Oval.) The sprinkler is clicking and flicking in a corner of the yard, and the earthy smell of the chookhouse mingles with the fragrance of ripe nectarines and damp grass. Already the mosquitoes are beginning to start their evening whine.

While it's still light Lulu calls everybody inside for the evening meal, which is always called tea. They have sliced cold meat (George carves) with boiled potatoes and salad and tomatoes and home-made pickles. Almost all the vegetables come from the kitchen garden. George says grace before they start eating. There is green jelly with custard for pudding.

When the dishes have been done they sit in the dining room and play cards – easy games for the children, like Snap and Old Maid. Afterwards Lulu occupies herself with darning and mending, while George reads the *Chronicle*. Glen takes *Cole's Funny Picture Book* to read in bed. He never tires of looking at the two pages that show grainy photographs of early types of aeroplanes.[2]

Needless to say, I have made most of this up. Perhaps there wasn't green jelly with custard; perhaps Glen didn't read in bed (although I'm sure he would have been familiar with those aeroplanes). But I suspect it isn't too far from the truth. These are the sorts of scenes a genre artist like Norman Rockwell would have loved to paint: idyllic scenes showing an ordinary, happy, stable suburban family.

Chapter 7

Forbes, New South Wales

'And then, of course,' my uncle tells me, 'there was Nancy.'

He says the name as if it's important, as if I should know it.

'Who was Nancy?' I ask.

'Nancy,' says Uncle David, and there is warmth in his voice, 'was the love of Glen's life.'

While Glen and his brothers grow up under the strict but loving eye of their mother and absorb by his quiet example the qualities of perseverance and courage from their father, a little girl is growing up on a rural property at Forbes, famous for its association with the bushranger Ben Hall, near Grenfell in New South Wales.

Her name is Nancy Priddle. Such a pretty, frilly, sunny, frivolous name. Not, I must add, that there was anything especially frivolous about Nancy, but she did start life with many gifts, not least the good fortune of being born into a loving, well-to-do, long-established country family – a family which, with its generous community spirit and prominence in local affairs, was remarkably similar to Glen's.

Nancy was born to Bertha and Sydney Priddle on 1 August 1923 at Nurse McClung's private hospital in

Grenfell. She was the youngest of three girls. Her sisters were Lorraine, who being eight years older was almost of a different generation, and June, to whom she was to become especially close. The family property, Birangan, would be her home for almost the next twenty years.

The first significant event in Nancy's life, although naturally she would not remember it, took place in March 1924, when Grenfell staged an unashamedly self-congratulatory festival to celebrate its pioneer days. It was called, with great cheeriness, 'Hop Back to Grenfell Week', and it was attended by the sort of crowds not seen since the gold rush. 'Grenfell has had many big days in the past', enthused the reporter for the *Sydney Morning Herald*, 'but never one equal to yesterday.'

The major feature of the opening celebrations was a procession *nearly a mile long*, headed by the police and followed by over a thousand children. Two wagons drawn by teams each of eighteen bullocks, 'wonderfully well driven', carried fifteen tons of wheat and fifteen tons of wool. After them came horse-drawn wagons and lorries loaded with primary produce – wheat, chaff, timber, lucerne and wool. A band queen, a country queen, a shire queen and a sports queen, all with their attendants, followed in cars decked with balloons and streamers and crepe-paper rosettes. A ceremonial arch decorated with wheat and oats straddled the main street, and the town was decorated with 'flags, signs, pine trees, and electric lights, well distributed'.

Among the many novelty events staged for the occasion was a Beautiful Baby competition. Not surprisingly, given the huge surge in local pride, it attracted many entrants, and from these eight-month-old Nancy was chosen. Prizes were also awarded – shockingly, it now seems – to the 'best looking schoolboy' and the 'best looking schoolgirl'. One can only hope that the field was large, so that the slight to those not selected was less painful.[1]

(I am reminded that my father, at the end of his final year in primary school, was given a prize for being 'the

'Beautiful Baby' Nancy with her mother in 1923

most gentlemanly boy in the school'. It was whispered that this horribly smarmy prize, a one-off, was dreamed up by my grandmother in association with a good friend on the school committee, to make up for the fact that he was not in the running for any other award. Whatever its source, I know that it caused my twelve-year-old father considerable anguish, not assuaged by the prize itself, which was the 1928 edition of *The Schoolboy's Annual.*)

Nancy suffered no such stigma. A portrait photograph in the Children's Pages of the *Sydney Mail*, captioned 'A Prize Baby', shows her being held by her mother in one of those side-and-back shots (Marcel-waved hair, rope of pearls) much favoured by society photographers. The light that falls flatteringly on her mother's hair turns Nancy's eyes to currants, her mouth to a small straight line. One plump little hand rests lightly on her mother's restraining arm.[2]

In March 1925 she was singled out again, this time at a children's fancy-dress ball organised by the Grenfell CWA. The hall 'presented a very gay and pretty scene', and festivities began, as usual, with a grand march. The judges had a hard task choosing the prize-winners. So much effort expended by all the contestants, so much determination to be original! Along with the more conventional costumes (swagmen, kewpie dolls, pierrots and fairies), children came cunningly disguised as powder-puffs and bonbons, gumnuts and mushrooms, and even, following a burst of parental imaginative creativity, as a crochet bag. Eighteen-month-old Nancy stole all hearts as a Balloon Girl in the 'Tiny Tots' section.

The Balloon Girl concept was given another airing at the Grenfell District School's Juvenile Ball just three years later – perhaps Bertha Priddle was too busy to be inventive – but this time it went unnoticed among the crowd of fairies and clowns and butterflies, soldiers and Red Cross nurses. Already there were hints of the Depression to come, with a special award for 'Cheapest Costume' (shared by Sunbeams, Minties, Flour and Tramp). Some costumes took their inspiration from Great Britain, still the revered Mother Country, with two Robin Redbreasts, a Colleen, two Highland Laddies and a Highland Lassie, and the ever popular Dick Whittington and his Cat. Flowers were as usual a pretty choice, with Chrysanthemum, Peach Blossom and Daffodil making their shy appearance. Coming way out of left field (but sadly unrewarded) was Wind Bag.[3]

As Nancy grows older, there are more fancy-dress frolics, Sunday School picnics, Christmas parties, sports days: the universally popular entertainments of country communities, based around school and church. All are described in some detail in the *Grenfell Record and Lachlan District Advertiser*, for reports of local activities are the bread-and-butter of regional newspapers, and people love to see their names in print.

Past copies of the *Grenfell Record* represent a perfect time capsule of country life and concerns in the 1920s, with plenty of attention given to matters of appeal to women. Side by side with advertisements for tractor oil, special horse sales, and sales of fat sheep and wethers, you will find advertisements for corsetry ('a dainty mode with smart uplift bust section of Swami Silk'), elastic-knit swimming costumes, Charmosan face powder ('You look YEARS YOUNGER and twice as pretty'), Arnott's milk-coffee biscuits ('refuse substitutes'), Aunt Mary's Baking

Nancy in 1927, aged three

Powder, De Witt's Kidney and Bladder Pills, and Goldenia Tea ('ensures palatable appreciation at all times'). There are also local cricket scores, church notices, advertisements for cheap railway trips or movies at the Royal Theatre (Adolphe Menjou in *The Great Lover*), auctions, council meetings, ganger's reports, Field Days, and reports on deaths, weddings and birthday parties. The post-war rural world, in fact, in microcosm.

Nancy's first school, the Driftway Public School, is typical of many single-teacher schools in farming areas that are a long way from major towns. Over the years many of them

Dressed for an outing: Nancy's sisters, Lorraine (left) and June, in about 1928

have closed down – my own, in country South Australia, included. The Driftway opens in 1928, but initially operates from a private house while the school building is being constructed. It is doll-house sized, a neat weatherboard with a pitched roof and two high windows. Nancy is among the first sixteen students. There she is in a blurry snapshot of the historic sixteen, stuffed into a tight drop-waisted school tunic worn, for warmth, over a pullover. Her knee-length socks are starting to slide downwards. A dark pudding-bowl hat is pulled down around her ears. Something is in her right hand, clutched firmly – a stick? A special stick? A knitting needle? Standing next to her, demure in a similar but paler hat, another little girl – her cousin, Margaret Priddle – holds out her skirt as if about to curtsy. For her the photograph is serious business. For Nancy, it seems, it's a bit of a joke, although I can't see if she's smiling: with the sun full on her face her features are almost obliterated. She has thrust her chin out, challenging the photographer, while the other children look down or away.[4]

I have a feeling that little Nancy could be a bit of a handful.

The new school's first Christmas Tree and Break-up Party is held in a local woolshed. There is a picnic tea, the children present 'a short entertainment', and Father Christmas makes an unexpected appearance. Among the prizes awarded there is one for demure Margaret Priddle, but none for Nancy. However, a special book prize, donated jointly by Nancy's mother and her aunt, is given to each of the sixteen pupils to mark the school's first year of operation.

In 1932 Nancy, now aged eight, goes to a Plain and Fancy Dress Ball to benefit the school fund.[5] It is held at Old

A professional photograph of Nancy, prettily posed at a dolls' tea party in 1929

Glenelg, the home of her generous and clearly prosperous uncle, Bert Priddle, who can offer a ballroom with a dance floor measuring 58 by 26 feet. The children are allowed to monopolise this, skidding and sliding on floorboards slick with French chalk, until ten o'clock, after which the adults have their more dignified turn. The over-excited children fall asleep in the back seats of cars or are tucked into beds hastily made up from rugs and overcoats while their parents dance the night away. I can see Nancy, drowsy in her Flower Girl costume (not a Balloon Girl this year) being picked up and carried to the family car in her father's arms.

That same year the school's Christmas party is again held at Bert Priddle's home. The hall is prettily decorated and *lighted by electricity*, and there is a Christmas tree 'heavily laden with gifts for young and old'.[6] As usual the school students present various concert items, to indulgent smiles and loud applause, after which prizes are awarded for academic performance. Still there is no prize for Nancy. Is she disappointed? Probably not: in almost any school there are some children regarded (occasionally with a degree of resentment) as 'brains', and the other children know all too well who they are. I don't think Nancy is one of these children. She may not be especially interested in schoolwork, nor does she seem to be especially gifted athletically. (Possibly unfairly, I come to this conclusion because her name doesn't appear in the results of events held at the 1933 school picnic and sports day, a day 'bright from start to finish' and filled with 'some very close and exciting' races.)[7]

As somebody for whom sporting success has always been an unachievable dream, I like Nancy more and more. I sense that she is the sort of child who is happy at home on the farm with her family and her pony and her pets; that she will take part in activities, in a good-natured sort of way, but isn't particularly competitive; that she is popular, a bit dreamy, and possibly, as is often the case with greatly loved, seldom-thwarted little girls, rather bossy. I can't forget that forward-thrust, challenging little face in the early school photograph. This is a child who is sure of herself, and secure in the love of those around her. That said, she must have worked harder in her later years at primary school, because at the 1933 Christmas Tree and Break-up Party she at last received recognition for her efforts.[8] The function (held again in Bert Priddle's spacious ballroom) began with six o'clock tea, after which Father Christmas – I'm guessing that it was Uncle Bert himself – arrived to give a present to each child from the toy-laden tree in the centre of the room. The children gave a concert of five items (song and drama), and then the prizes were given. The final award of the evening, a special prize for 'Improvement', went to Nancy. It would have been a moment for her to cherish, and for parents and friends to acknowledge with especially warm applause: day-dreamer Nancy, regarded with affection by all, had shown that she could apply herself. For a child to whom study doesn't come easily, reward for effort is sweet indeed.

Nancy was practical, though. In 1934, her last year at the Driftway, she won first prize in the Girls' division for her carefully tended school garden plot. (I expect that, as was usual then, the girls grew flowers and the boys grew manlier vegetables.) Nancy the Balloon Girl, Nancy the Flower Girl would have wanted her garden above all to be pretty. She would have chosen bright flowers, but those sturdy enough to weather heat and dryness – golden marigolds and white marguerites, blue cornflowers, blowsy pink zinnias, snapdragons that fastened around your finger with soft mouths, spires of hollyhocks: an English cottage garden in miniature, under the hot Australian sun. She would have put time into improving the earth, digging in poultry manure from home, weeding, lugging water from the school rainwater tank in a big watering-can. Even as a child, her natural impulse was for tending, for nurturing.

A month later Nancy was one of just three students from her school to pass the Primary Final Examination and gain entrance to the Secondary Department of the Grenfell Intermediate High School.[9] She was on her way.

Chapter 8

Gathering Clouds

Leap forward eighteen months or so to 1936. Twelve-year-old Nancy is in high school, and Glen has just turned fourteen. Neither, obviously, has the slightest idea that the other exists, but in the mysterious way that life works, the first steps towards their meeting are being put in place.

It is nearly Easter, and the front page of the *Advertiser* for 3 April is full of holiday bargains from Adelaide's several department stores. Confusingly, John Martin's is inviting customers to 'Bring the kiddies into BUNNYLAND for a ride on Rudolph, the reindeer'. Bunnyland (a curiously inappropriate name, given that the feral rabbit is in plague proportions throughout country South Australia) is 'the most unique, and merriest place in town', where lucky children can meet Miss Betty Bunny, and ride on the reindeer, who, mysteriously, has 'just arrived'. Birks is advertising delicious meals in its Piccadilly Restaurant, which also serves Lenten Dishes at popular prices; an Easter egg accompanies the sale of each pair of children's felt rabbit slippers. (I remember, suddenly, that I once had just such a pair, the toes adorned with rabbit faces with black beads sewn on for eyes.)

Turn to page 33 of this newspaper, and there is Glen's name, in print, in a column headed 'Model Flying Clubs'. It is reported that the meeting on 30 March of the Kensington Model Aeroplane Club took place in the fairly cramped conditions of the Kensington Park Methodist Church hall.

Indoor flying was indulged in after the business was finished, and Jack Bartholomew and Jack Black, with microfilm models, gained good times considering the size of the hall. Don Leatheby, Roger Freeman, Glen Murrie, and Maurice Boot flew all-Balsa speed models. A flying meeting will be held tomorrow afternoon, weather permitting, at Stanley street, Burnside.

Glen was always more mechanically minded than his brothers, but here is proof of his particular fascination with flying. Given that he has just turned fourteen, it is probably an interest that has been forming for some years. Boys, especially, are often obsessed by planes and trains and cars at quite an early age. Was Glen's interest increased still further by the knowledge that his great-grandmother had taken to the air in her eighties? Did he especially notice the veterans of the four Australian Flying Corps squadrons, only a small group, marching on Anzac Day? Was he the sort of boy who watched birds soaring through the air and wondered, looking down at his own earthbound feet, how flight was possible? All these things may have played a part. It's likely, too, that Glen was impressed by the daring exploits of the great Australian aviator Sir Charles Kingsford Smith. Kingsford Smith had been for many years a charismatic public figure, but recently his name was even more in the news because he had died on 8 November 1935, when his plane, the *Lady Southern Cross*, had disappeared off the coast of Burma.[1]

Perhaps, like so many boys, Glen dreams of following in the steps of his hero, but for now he just wants to understand the mechanics of flying. I can see him sitting at the kitchen table at Hazelwood Park, cutting out the balsa sections, patiently working out the construction of a wing, checking the balance of the tail. (This image morphs into one of my own son, just a couple of years younger, putting together a model glider in an almost visible fug of dope and wood glue.)

In 1936 it is eighteen years since the end of the First World War, and the Depression is over, but already new and even more sinister shadows are beginning to lengthen and darken over Europe. Most Australians are still unaware of them, or choose to ignore them. They are working hard to make their country prosperous again. Following the dual disasters of war and the financial chaos that engulfed the world after the collapse of Wall Street in 1929, the mid to late 1930s appear in retrospect to be a time of innocence and fun. But there are indications that the lengthening shadows are now touching Australia.

It is likely that Glen read this April edition of the newspaper that contains his name. I wonder if he also read these anxious letters to the editor. This one, from a mother:

Sir – I was surprised and horrified at our principal colleges – St. Peter's, Prince Alfred, King's, and Scotch Colleges – favouring military training for our boys. It's sad to find that we have gone back twenty years in education. If there's anything we need, it is the higher education of Christianity, so that our boys can be trained to manage this troubled world in a nobler spirit, than by resorting to war. Military training breeds war. There's no getting away from that. Another batch of young boys is getting ready and the fathers who should know better are helping to hasten on what every mother deplores. The mothers feel there's no glamour in war. We suffered too much in the last one to bear to go through another . . . – I am, Sir, &c.

Or this one, from a volunteer with the Royal Australian Naval Reserve:

Sir – Messrs. Bills and Beck in your paper of March 38 ask if we can ever fully defend our country. Do they imply that if we cannot adequately defend all of it, we should not try to defend it at all? What would the Australian public think of a decision to abolish all defence training and do away with our navy, army, and air force, simply because we could not afford to make a thorough job of our defence at present? Would we be relieved in mind if our taxes were decreased, and we lived like helpless natives, hoping against hope that no land-hungry nation would observe our plight and see an outlet for its overflow of humanity? . . . It does not seem patriotic to me to suggest that we have no right to keep this continent for our own kin. Our pioneers suffered great hardships to gain it for us, and we should show that we are worthy of it, and prepared to safeguard it. . . . It is the duty of every youth to acquire at least some knowledge of defence, and for this reason I favour the reintroduction of compulsory training. . . . We Australians dread the thought of war, but by becoming defenceless we would invite it. – I am, Sir, &c.

Or this, beneath the by-line 'Be Prepared':

The thanks of all people who wish to retain their British inheritance is due to the headmasters of St. Peter's, Prince Alfred, and Scotch Colleges for stating that they are in favour of military training, as it inculcates discipline and improves the young man's physique: even Scout law is a great help in making boys manly. There are too many 'cissies' who would leave the defence of their hearth to the class of men who fought in the last war. Why should the patriots fight for the shirkers? If a country is worth living in, it is worth being prepared to defend.

With Australia poised between airy confidence and disturbing rumours of trouble ahead, and the possible future role of young men hanging in the balance, the Murrie brothers continue their carefree existence. Their baby sister Gwenyth is now seven, and despite Lulu's private dream of having twin girls, there will be no more children. They are a solid, affectionate family unit, bolstered by economic security and a vast and supportive network of relatives. The boys often stay with aunts and uncles who have farms: with Lulu's sister, Merle Correll, and her family at Clinton Centre on Yorke Peninsula, or with 'Uncle Will and Aunt Em' – my grandparents – at their Eden Valley property, Avon Brae. The Vigars and the Murries are close. During the summer holidays both families usually go down to Port Elliot, on the south coast of the Fleurieu Peninsula, for Christmas. My grandmother owns a holiday house (half of an attached cottage, Djin-Djin, right beside the railway line); the Murries usually camp on the foreshore of Horseshoe Bay, next to the bowling green.

This photograph, taken possibly at Djin-Djin in the mid to late 1930s, is rare in that it shows both my grandparents. Their older daughter Kathleen is at the back, on the right, and Elizabeth is in front, sitting next to her father. The other woman and the two children have not been identified. I don't know where my father was: perhaps he took the photo

Port Elliot, with its air of slightly decayed British gentility, is the sort of place childhood dreams are made of. Horseshoe Bay, a curve of golden sand contained by rocky headlands, is made for scampering in and out of lightly curling and frothing waves, with just enough undertow to be mildly exciting. Further out to sea there are some small rugged islets, and after a specially big breaker you can see creamy white foam pouring like custard over the rounded rock known as the Christmas Pudding. Seagulls squawk and steal sandwich crusts, fishermen big and small cluster on the old wooden jetty, children construct moated marvels of sandcastles decorated with seaweed pennants and rows of pipis. There is an entrancing scent of salt and iodine and fish; the air is salty, too, and fresh on your face. When you go to the kiosk for ice creams you have to race through the hot sand to avoid scorching your bare feet. The pain of legs and arms and backs afflicted by sunburn, and only partly soothed by vinegar or lanoline, is valiantly borne.

Above the beach is the memorial garden with its neat beds of roses and blazing summer flowers, and (inspiring reflection and melancholy) the rows of Norfolk Island pines, each tree accompanied by a plaque bearing the name of a soldier who gave his life in the First World War. Everybody still hopes, and possibly even believes, that there will never be another one.

Chapter 9

Head of the River

All George and Lulu's children went to Marryatville Primary School, the school Lulu herself had attended earlier. By 1936 the twins were enrolled at the new Urrbrae Agricultural High School, which had been established in 1932 with an innovative curriculum focused on agriculture and farming technology. Glen was a student at Adelaide High School, a public school renowned for high academic achievement, when he was awarded a half-fee open scholarship to Scotch College in the foothills suburb of Mitcham.

Scotch College has always been familiar to me, because it's my father's old school. He used to own a framed etching of the main building with a little enamelled Scotch badge (a red lion on gold, superimposed on the blue and white Saltire) stuck beneath it. Perhaps the etching was a gift from his parents: I don't think he would have bought it himself, as his school memories were not especially pleasant. He also owned a framed group photograph of the Scotch boarders, in which he (first on the left, second row from the front) cuts a despairing little figure. Jacket crumpled, shoulders hunched, he glowers darkly at the photographer. Looking at this photo, my mother once observed that he looked like the unhappiest little boy in the school. When he was called back to the farm at the age of fifteen to help his father, it must have seemed a blessed release. I can imagine, based on my own experience of being schooled away from home, the deep loneliness he felt as a shy, not especially sociable child, estranged from his parents, his sisters, his beloved Avon Brae. In his final year at the school he was taken out of the boarding house and placed as a private boarder in the home of a woman who lived in Watson Street, Fullarton. It was at this point in his life, on Tuesday 29 September 1931, that he distinguished himself by saving two schoolmates from drowning after a freak beach accident – a feat that earned him the Royal Humane Society Medal for Bravery.[1]

My father was a quick-witted, intelligent man, but he was not gifted academically. His conventional school studies bored him and left him floundering. His writing was untidy, his ability to organise limited, his degree of application minimal. The need to study subjects of no interest to him whatsoever reduced him to angry frustration. Once, when my brother and I were playing down the creek at Avon Brae, we found in a pile of dumped rubbish a mildewed copy of *Julius Caesar* with our father's name inked on the flyleaf and surrounded by smeared inkblots, trial signatures and cartoon faces. Small for his age and sensitive (he hated being teased), quick to anger and not particularly good at sport, he was far from being the sort of rounded student that private schools pride themselves on producing.

Glen, on the other hand, was exactly that sort of student. He fitted perfectly into the Scotch tradition. Six years younger than my father, he excelled on just about every level. After a rather dispiriting academic result in 1938 he set himself to working even harder at his studies, and in 1939 he matriculated with passes in five subjects (English,

Maths 1, Maths 2, Chemistry and Physics). He had played the piano since primary school, and at Scotch he was considered good enough to be made school pianist. Later he also played the pedal organ with the school's recently formed orchestra. He was a member of the debating society. Tall, strong and athletic, he was also, as my uncle mildly expressed it, 'quite a good rower'.

Even when their children were small, George and Lulu had encouraged them to take part in sporting pursuits. The boys played football and cricket and tennis, and all the children were capable swimmers. Glen enjoyed cricket: he was a reliable wicketkeeper and in spite of being right-handed he was a useful left-hand bat. Gwenyth, like her father, proved to be especially good at tennis.

As well as playing sport and taking piano lessons, Glen was for several years a Scout with the Linden Park group, and the many outdoor activities that were part of Scouting helped to develop both his practical abilities and his interest in the world of nature. And like most boys then, he was always on his pushbike. Once he secured a school holiday job as a telegram delivery boy with the Burnside Post Office, a neat red-brick building on the eastern side of Glynburn Road. On one particular Saturday his task was to take congratulatory wedding telegrams to a reception being held at Beaumont, in the foothills. Each telegram had to be delivered as soon as it was received, and the multiple trips this involved, up a very steep hill, would have tested his fitness to the utmost.

Unlike my father, Glen was not a boarder at Scotch, not an outcast from his own country. He left his Hazelwood Park home every morning with his brothers, and the three

The Murrie boys (from left, David, Glen and Bruce) and Gwenyth with the family's cat. Glen is wearing the Scotch College uniform, so this photograph could have been taken in either 1938 or 1939

boys cycled to school together. The twins (both over six feet tall by their mid-teens) finished their journey at Urrbrae on Cross Road, and Glen continued on up gently inclining Fullarton Road to Scotch, a total ride of about six miles. There was little traffic about then, and much of what is now built over was open farmland, with cow paddocks and wheatfields. Mitcham was still essentially the village it had been in the early years of settlement. It consisted of a few large villas, churches, a scattering of smaller cottages, a general store, a 'village green' with a bandstand, a primary school, an institute, hotels and shops.[2] On rising land overlooking the village was an imposing gothic sandstone building, Torrens Park House, which had been built in 1853 as the private home of Sir Robert Torrens. Although he was briefly the third premier of South Australia, Torrens became much more famous for having devised the revolutionary system of transferring real estate (the *Real Property Act of 1858*) known as the Torrens Title and now used all over the world. Torrens Park House was later owned by the Barr Smith family, and in 1919 it became the main building of Scotch College. The school was officially incorporated in 1922.

Glen started at Scotch in March 1938: first term began late that year because the poliomyelitis epidemic that had broken out in 1937 was still causing concern. The new boy settled in quickly. It wasn't long before the school's rowing coach, Lyn Davis, recognised his talents, and soon he was given a berth in the Scotch Eight. At Adelaide High School Glen had rowed Bow in a four-oared 'tub slide' crew for the Head of the River, and in the 1938 Scotch Eight he again rowed Bow, a position requiring strength, quick thinking, and a level head. The two front oarsmen, Bow and Two, are largely responsible for maintaining the direction and stability of the boat – not always an easy task, as the bow is the section most liable to pitching.

Glen was more than just 'quite a good rower'. In 1939 he was a senior member of the rowing club, elected Vice-Captain of Boats, and was rowing at Five, in the so-called 'engine room' or powerhouse section, where the strongest rowers are positioned. In his critique of the Eight, published in the school magazine for 30 May 1939, his coach noted approvingly Glen's improvement as an oarsman: 'Has been working hard to eliminate a tendency to stiffness in his hand and body movement; has ironed out this fault.' (As I

Glen in his white First Eight blazer, which is now in the Scotch College archives

am to discover, this sort of thoroughness is typical of Glen's attitude to everything he does.) Together with the other crew members, he was awarded full colours for rowing.

For decades the Head of the River has been one of the standout fixtures on the South Australian school calendar. In the 1930s it was held on the Torrens Lake, and it was a much smaller affair than today's huge gathering at West Lakes. Only four schools – Prince Alfred's, Saint Peter's,

Scotch and Adelaide High – had rowing crews, and the Head of the River itself, the final race between the two winning Eights after heats, was almost always fought out between the two oldest, Saint's and Prince's. In 1939 there was a good chance that this might change. With its strong crew, brilliant rowing coach and dedicated training regime, the word was out that it could be Scotch's turn to win the Gosse Shield. When the boys completed their training with a test race against the State King's Cup crew, acquitting themselves remarkably well, Scotch rose further in the stakes as favourite. 'Adelaide in former years has not shown the excitement and fervour that usually surrounds the Head of the River in Melbourne or Sydney,' wrote a reporter for the *News*, 'but this year promises to be an exception.'[3]

It's 15 April 1939, a week before the Saturday of the regatta, and training has intensified, with the crews taking to the river every afternoon after school. People break the trip home after work to watch from the banks of the Torrens. 'Are you ready? *Row!*' scream the shrill voices of the young coxes. Crews sweat and strain, ducks scatter, spectators armed with binoculars stand on the Morphett Street bridge to assess styles and prospects. Will Scotch win the coveted Gosse Shield for the first time since its establishment in 1934? Will Prince's defeat the odds to triumph again, and make it a hat trick? Can Saint's overcome its unfortunate start to the season (half the team down with measles and missing training) and rise to its usual standard? What about Adelaide High – might it be the dark horse in this highly anticipated race?

On Friday 21 April, in his final discussion of the form

shown by the competing schools, the *Advertiser*'s Rowing Correspondent writes:

If form, times, and watermanship mean anything it appears that Scotch College and Adelaide High School, outsiders in these regattas in recent years because of the paucity of oarsmen and the lightness of their crews, will fight out the final tomorrow down the difficult 1,000 [yards]of the Henley course.

Scotch College is chosen to win Head-of-the-River this year. The victory of either Scotch College or Adelaide High would be extremely popular in rowing circles, for these schools have battled tenaciously in the past year and now appear to have the chance of gaining their reward.

Scotch College appears to be the best crew on the river. It has been rowing together for over four months, and thanks to Mr. Lyn Davis, the coach, whose son is a member of the crew, this ultra-light eight is as fit as a mentor could make them, and as fast as any school crew of 10 st 2 lb. could be. Their time over the course on Wednesday, when they rowed a losing race against the King's Cup crew, who have them 2 st. 7 lb. a man, stamped Scotch as a class crew. A fortnight at Mannum in January helped the crew's physique, and another holiday on the same water at Easter polished them up.

Excitement at Scotch is reaching fever pitch. Nothing matters but the contest: even the teachers allow a little unaccustomed levity. On the eve of the regatta the boys, kept only slightly in check by prefects, leap and dance as they practise their war cry:

Wazza, wazza, wazza, wazza, wazza, wazza woo
Blue and gold, blue and gold, ever gold and blue.

The twenty-second of April is a cool, crisp, sunny day, the sky vast and blue: perfect boating weather. The Torrens Lake sparkles with millions of tiny stars; up close, the greenish river water gives off a dank, swampy smell. The crowd is noisy and high-spirited. Boys in school uniform dart everywhere, bright with exertion and excitement. Coloured streamers strung from trees and poles and marquees drift in the light breeze – royal blue for Saint's, black for Adelaide High, blue and gold for Scotch, red for Prince's. Ribbons in bunches and rosettes adorn boater hats and lapels. Women are dressed as if for a fashion parade, for this is one of Adelaide's glamour sporting events of the year, a chance to show both personal status and school loyalty. The newspapers' fashion columns will detail the colourful outfits worn, down to the last detail of stitching and the last hat feather. *Smart autumn frocking* is expected, and that expectation must be more than fulfilled.

People gather early to find the best vantage points. They throng the riverbank as far as the Morphett Street bridge and cram themselves into the newly erected stands that provide seating. Under the trees near the kiosk long tables are covered with white tablecloths. Picnickers spread their rugs in the shade of poplar trees, and willows trail their green fronds in the water. Most of the ducks have been shooed away, but a few still dive and dabble near a muddy stretch of shore.

The Murries are there on the bank, George and Lulu, the twins and Gwenyth, even the grandmothers, warmly rugged up against the cold. Lulu, always a neat and elegant dresser, is wearing her best hat. The whole family is fiercely proud of Glen, and by extension his school. Their eyes are constantly drawn to the river and the distant crews in their white shorts and singlets, trying to spot their own boy among the many. They know how much the Head of the River means to him: it means almost as much to them. They appear relaxed and unconcerned, but the anticipation is almost unbearable.

The minor events – the under-fifteens, the under-sixteens, the tub slides and the old collegians' race – are already over. It's time for the first heat of the Eights: Saint's against Scotch. Saint's has drawn north side, and Scotch south.

To the relief of Scotch and Adelaide High, the regatta's two lightweight crews, the breeze, which strengthened earlier, has died again. The wind is now down course.

The crowd tenses, waiting for the gun.

Scotch starts smoothly, and immediately takes the lead. The crowd goes wild. Under the bridge the two boats go. Now Scotch is nearly a length ahead, and the crew are rowing like veterans. Then – disaster. The Scotch cox has picked the wrong target of the two placed at the finish to give the coxes their line. Suddenly the Scotch Eight is right over in Saint's water. A hundred yards from the finish the cox realises his mistake and brings Scotch sharply back to the right target. They skim over the line just a length ahead of Saint's. The gun fires twice: the south side crew has won. It was a near thing, though. The Scotch boys know they narrowly missed being disqualified. They slump over their oars, adrenaline pumping.

The Prince's Eight wins the second heat to loud cheering from those decked in red ribbons. They know they are the

**The Scotch Eight at the Head of the River in April 1939.
Glen is fourth from left, rowing at Five**

underdogs, but they are buoyed by the thought of a hat trick. Suddenly it seems possible, even probable.

In the break before the main event, the crowd mills about. Girls compare outfits and repair their make-up (as reported in the evening paper, with a clumsy attempt at humour) '*in the full view of the passers-by* adding colour and powder to their young faces with a zeal worthy of the highest domestic duty'. There are shouted greetings and laughter. Picnicking families link up with friends. Discreet flirting goes on as schoolgirls meet schoolboys burnished with reflected glory from their respective crews. The atmosphere is part carnival, part school pride, part social gathering. Queues at the kiosk grow longer, and there is brisk trade in soft drinks and Amscol's Dandy ice creams. Sporadic chanting from cheer squads becomes louder and more frenetic.

At last the crews of the two competing Eights are called

to the start. They receive last-minute instructions from their coaches. The boys grin nervously, attempt to joke. They jig up and down, flex their arms, loosen their shoulders. Tension, combined with a chill in the air, makes them shiver. Glen glances briefly at the bank, hoping to see his family. He knows they are there somewhere, knows they are sending him silent messages of support. The noise of the crowd seems to come from a long way off.

It's time. The rival boats are lined up, the sleek wooden shells bobbing gently on the torpid river water. The rowers are poised, leaning slightly forward, oars ready. The sun shines. The crowd holds its breath.

Bang goes the starter's gun, and now the crowd is galvanised. 'Come on, Scotch!' 'Come on, Prince's!' 'Go it, Scotch!' 'P-A-C! P-A-C!' The chanting of *Wazza, wazza, wazza, wazza!* is all but lost in the hubbub.

After the drama of the first heat, the final is uneventful. Scotch leads the red crew easily, all the way. When they win, by three-quarters of a length, the crowd is euphoric. The cheering can be heard as far away as North Terrace.

In his report on 24 April the *Advertiser*'s Rowing Correspondent describes the winning Eight as 'Living up to the high reputation it has earned as one of the best and neatest school crews seen on the river for some years'. They rowed, he writes, 'as if they were enjoying a practice spin':

No appearance of work, joy in each stroke, and steady recovery down the slide gave the appearance of almost leisureliness, the hallmark of a good crew. Prince's gallantly hung on to their opponent all the way up the straight, but they could make little impression.

Accompanying this report is a photograph that shows the victorious crew at the Elder Park rotunda, after Mrs Gosse has presented them with the Gosse Shield. They are the heroes of the hour, the focus of all attention. They look slightly overwhelmed, as if they still can't quite believe their success, but they wave their arms enthusiastically as they give three cheers for Mrs Gosse. The shield in its impressive frame is held in place for the photographer by F. Trembath, Stroke of the Eight, and J. Fearn. Standing directly behind the shield, his waving arm a blur, is Glen. He wears a white turtle-necked pullover and the Scotch navy-blue blazer with its distinctive gold pinstripe. Even in the black-and-white photo, he glows.

What is he thinking as he joins in the cheering? What

The victorious Eight give three cheers after the presentation of the Gosse Shield, with the Elder Park rotunda in the background. Glen is standing behind the shield

is he feeling? Elation and excitement, certainly; pride, and the knowledge that he has played his part in an achievement that will be remembered down the years as one of his school's finest. A sense, too, that he has done his family proud: that their financial sacrifice to send him to Scotch (although the half-scholarship has certainly helped) has been in some sense rewarded. And a sensation of physical accomplishment. On this day, at this moment, he is probably healthier and stronger and more resilient than he has ever been in his life. His heart beats firm and steady, warm blood pulses through his veins, his head is clear, his muscles are like whipcord. He could row that race all over again and never feel it. He is bursting with energy, a perfectly functioning human being, ready for anything. More than that, he is an essential and valued member of a team. He has something to contribute, and he has done just that.

He is just seventeen, and in less than five months Australia will be at war.

Chapter 10

Jackeroos

In his final year at school Glen turned his love of mechanics, a love he shared with my father, to good use. He bought a wreck of an old Wolseley for £10 and, with the help of a cousin, Gordon Murrie, dismantled it and rebuilt it into a serviceable car. It was in this car, early in 1940, that Glen, nearly eighteen, and his younger brother Bruce drove up to Avon Brae to begin their lives as farmers. The twins had both passed their Leaving exams, and as a result David had won a scholarship from Urrbrae to attend Roseworthy Agricultural College. He would spend three more years as a student, ending up as dux of his year.

It may seem curious that all three brothers wanted to go on the land, as they were born and raised in the suburbs, but it isn't altogether surprising. The family's rural background was a strong influence, and because the boys had often spent school holidays on the properties of country relatives, they had a fair idea of what farming was all about. To give them more hands-on experience, particularly in sheep farming, it was decided that Glen and Bruce would live at Avon Brae and work for Uncle Will and Aunt Em.

My father, Len, was about to leave home to join the RAAF, and this meant that his father needed help to work the property. Employing Glen and Bruce, at the going rate for jackeroos of full lodgings and a wage of ten shillings a week, provided an ideal solution. It was a low-risk enterprise. My grandparents would have accepted without question the suitability and sound work ethic of the two boys they were prepared to take on. It was a matter of blood, of family. Of 'good stock'.

My father had written to the RAAF on 15 January 1940 to volunteer his services ('I am desirous of enlisting in the Royal Australian Air Force' he wrote with barely disguised eagerness). He was tested for his aptitude as a mechanic on 23 February and was informed less than two weeks later that his application had been accepted.[1]

The record of my father's enlistment states that he was a grazier and had worked on his father's property for eleven years. The 'eleven years' – in fact it was only eight, full-time – is telling. Life on a medium-sized farm might be cosily familiar, and in his own way he loved it (in later years he often spoke passionately of the need to have 'your own piece of dirt'), but it was also stultifying. I have never been entirely sure that my father wanted to be a farmer. Unlike Glen and his brothers, it wasn't a choice for him, but more a matter of expectation. As the only son, there was no question that he would follow in his father's footsteps. But still something in him kicked against the pricks. In March 1940, further underlining his desire for independence, he had become engaged to be married.

The speed with which my father enlisted speaks of a huge and hungry need for adventure, a need to break free. (Clearly the presence of a fiancée didn't appear to him to be a particular tie.) He may have hoped that the air force would provide him with the excitement that was lacking

My father in air force uniform, 1940

in his life. It is likely, too, that after working together for so long, he and his father were aware of areas where they didn't get along, where they had different ideas or rubbed each other up the wrong way. My grandfather was a kind and gentle man who belonged to a different, pre-mechanical age. Born in 1879, he was descended from a long line of Somerset yeoman farmers going back to the time of the Norman conquest. He was sober and careful, but open to new ways, too: he was one of the first graziers locally to use superphosphate, for example, and in 1929 he won a silver cup from the Superphosphate Association of South Australia for the most improved pasture. In everything he did he was sensible and methodical, his actions and decisions weighted by practical experience handed down by generations of farming forebears. My father, on the other hand, was impatient, and because of this he tended to be careless – 'slapdash', my mother would have said. He was a product of the mechanical age, and in his heart he always preferred cars and planes to sheep.

When my father enlisted in the RAAF he was twenty-three, and he had seen comparatively little of life. He was taken on as a trainee flight mechanic and sent to the recruitment depot at Laverton in Victoria on 1 April 1940. I am sure that he set off with an eager heart and great expectations. He was soon transferred to the Maintenance Wing of No. 2 Squadron at Point Cook.

During his training my father showed himself to be a capable mechanic, very likely even a good one, but his time in the air force was abruptly terminated. It turned out that he suffered from thyrotoxicosis, a condition that gave him 'total incapacity as an airman'. He was hospitalised for several weeks, and discharged as medically unfit on 28 April 1941.

My father's war service lasted for just one year and twenty-seven days, but it was to shape his life, for it was during this time that he met the woman who would become his wife, and my mother. They met at a dance for 'lonely airmen', a dance she went to reluctantly because she had a bad cold, and only after a friend had persuaded her that she simply had to attend because there weren't enough women.

So, because she believed it was her duty, she went. ('I don't know why he even looked at me,' she told me, once. 'I had the most awful red nose.')

Had she been a lazier, more selfish, less stoical woman, I should not be writing these words.

Adelaide in early 1940 seems to be still relatively unaffected by what is happening overseas. A typical copy of the *Advertiser* from this time spruiks cricket bats at special reduced prices, 'Kiddies' Beach Suits' of printed cotton in nursery designs, and men's woollen bathers. Easter brides are advised to take advantage of Cravens' special offer to furnish three rooms for £41 10s or to lay-by a four-piece walnut bedroom suite for nineteen guineas. Closer investigation shows an advertisement for 'Soldiers' knitting wool' at ninepence-halfpenny a skein, '. . . you have no excuse now for not starting knitting for the soldiers!' and a same-day hosiery repair service for 'single ladders only'. Patriotic activities, and the need for small personal economies, are beginning to show, and concern about the war is deepening. A five-valve dual-wave radio for only £6 19s 6d promises to bring 'War News direct from European Countries!!'. At the same time, people are keeping themselves cheerful. The movie houses are showing all the latest hits from Hollywood. *The Cisco Kid and the Lady* provides plenty of amusement, while *Goodbye Mr Chips*, with Robert Donat and Greer Garson, offers the chance to luxuriate in sentimental tears. For the more sophisticated romantic, Fred Astaire and Ginger Rogers star in *The Story of Vernon and Irene Castle*.

Small ads offer learn-to-dance lessons, Brylcreem ('gives hair a manly appearance'), crooning contests and a novice dancing championship. Twenty ostrich chicks are on show at the zoo, together with a free circus featuring a lion. War dominates the news pages, but Lady Kitty's Social News contains the usual gushingly detailed descriptions of parties and fashion. Letters to the editor deal with matters as diverse as the Soviet invasion of Finland, conscription, the menace of motorists dashing past stationary tramcars, the supply of intoxicants to soldiers, and the bitter taste of factory-made butter. A book titled *The Joke's On Hitler* is reviewed: 'Hitler inspires some rather obvious satire', writes the reviewer, acidly.[2]

In the same newspaper it is reported that the Director of RAAF Recruiting, Sir Donald Cameron, has arrived in Adelaide to organise next month's opening of the Empire Air Training Scheme.[3] He has now visited all five of the mainland capital cities. Stressing the need for Allied air supremacy in Europe and the magnitude of the Training Scheme, he says that he is 'tremendously impressed' with the enthusiasm shown by the men in all Australian States to serve their country in the RAAF. 'Young men are keen to join', he is quoted as saying.

My father's enlistment pre-dated Sir Donald Cameron's visit by a month, and this alone indicates the alacrity with which he joined up. It is impossible to say whether Glen's eagerness to join the RAAF was inspired by my father's example, or by Sir Donald's visit, or (and most likely) by his own great desire to be involved with those marvellous flying machines that had fascinated him for so long. There's no doubt that he was motivated, too, by a strong sense that joining up was 'the right thing to do'. Like my father, he probably also longed for excitement, and the excitement of flying beat any adventure that might be promised by being a footslogger in the PBI ('poor bloody infantry'). The air force was always the romantic service. RAAF servicemen in their blue uniforms were known, either disparagingly or admiringly, as Blue Orchids.

I see them now, Glen and Bruce, arriving at Avon Brae in Glen's restored Wolseley to begin their careers as farmers. What are their feelings? Some excitement, certainly; perhaps a little nervousness, but not very much, because Uncle Will and Aunt Em are family – the boys have been here before, as welcome guests, and their two families have spent many summers together at the beach. So at first it must seem, incongruously, a little as if they are going on holiday.

The car passes over the bridge that crosses the South Rhine, as the winding rocky creek is grandly named.[4] It climbs the hill, slowing a little as it reaches the top, and turns right at the homestead gates. Now in second gear, it rumbles past the dark, shaggy pines, past the hedge. It follows the curve of the driveway, stops at the side of the house. Glen and Bruce get out and go up the veranda steps – one, two.

Uncle Will, who one day will be my grandfather, opens one of the double doors adorned with Great-Aunt Charlotte's beautiful purple-and-green leadlight irises, and the boys are welcomed inside.

There they are, in the dining room. Len, the young man who will become my father, is there, too, as his departure date is still several weeks away. My future aunts are absent. By now Kathleen is married and has two babies, and Elizabeth is in Town training to be a Mothercraft nurse.

I remember vividly the dining room as it was then, five years before I was born, because it was unchanged for years afterwards.

The carpet square has a pattern of orange and yellow and tan autumn leaves, and the wood of the floor that borders it is dark with old varnish and years of polish. A picture rail running around the walls supports a huge Victorian etching framed in bird's-eye maple. Its title, written in fine copperplate, is 'English Merrymaking in the Olden Time'. The fireplace has a fumed oak surround with a shelf and a small oval mirror. Len leans casually against the mantel, smoking, flicking the ash into the cold fireplace. He is very much on his home ground, very much the more experienced older cousin. He doesn't offer around his pack of cork-tipped Craven A, because he knows the Murries don't smoke or drink.

The kitchen with its big cream coke-fuelled Aga stove is the centre of the house, but niceties must be upheld, and the evening meal is served in the dining room. My grandmother will have made an effort for Lulu's boys. She will have prepared something nourishing and filling – a hearty roast, or a brown stew, or curried sausages with plentiful mashed potato. She is a practical woman who knows how much young men eat, but she is thrifty, too. At shearing time she will cook separate meals for family and for shearers, using butter for the family and dripping for the workmen. Agee jars of biscuits on the pantry shelf are plainly labelled, in her firm handwriting, *Shearers*.

When the meal is over, there is a friendly but down-to-earth discussion with Uncle Will (a man of few words) and cousin Len (a man of more than a few words) about the work the new jackeroos will be expected to do. After that it's early bedtime. The working day starts with milking at six o'clock. The boys don't go down the hall to what will one day be my room. They are family, but they are now also employees, so it's appropriate that their bedroom should be the sleep-out. It has been divided into two small rooms which will be their quarters for the duration of their employment. It is much more Spartan accommodation than their room back in Hazelwood Park. They will discover that in winter time neither the louvres nor the flywire will do anything to keep the chilly air at bay.

That first night they will lie awake for a while on their narrow iron beds, listening to the profound depth of the country silence, a silence like no other.

Chapter 11

The Right Decision

Glen may have wanted to become a farmer, but his interest in flying had never waned. With the onset of war he had given serious thought to joining the RAAF – a thought he had already mentioned to his parents, with predictably negative results. Some time after starting his farming apprenticeship at Avon Brae, he tried again, this time putting his request in a letter. It has been preserved in an envelope on which is written, in George Murrie's neat and distinctive hand, 'Glen's letter asking for permission to enlist'. It is dated 12 May 1940.

Dear Mother and Father, the letter begins,

I expect you remember that about eight or nine weeks ago I asked you only half seriously whether you could give me your permission to enlist in the Royal Australian Air Force. Well Mother since then I have not stopped wanting or thinking about it. What I want is your permission to join the R.A.A.F. On reading this you will probably say, 'Oh Glen is too young, he does not realise what he is doing' or 'No, I could not think of letting him go.' But Mother I do, I have been praying about it and asking God to help me come to a decision and now this new turn of events [presumably he is referring to the German offensive against the Western Front, with the invasion of Luxembourg, France, Belgium and the Netherlands] has convinced me that I ought to go. Every day it has been on my mind. I expect you think I am silly writing like this but really I do feel I ought to go, so Mother don't just say what I said above but sleep on it for a couple of nights & give it your earnest consideration, will you? If I did enlist I would not be called up for a year or more, so think it over Mum. It has been hard for me to write this Mother & Dad, but I think you can arrive at the right decision.

Well now for something more cheery. Today is Mother's day and I expect you received the little gift we sent you safely. I hope you like it Mother.

We have been very busy lately with the pigs. Within the last week we have had 30 little pigs born and expect more today. They are pretty little things. We had bad luck this morning though, a mother had 11 little ones last night and must have lain on 8 of them & killed them.

We have also been busy going around the sheep and tailing. The lamb percentage is very good so far but lately we have lost some lovely lambs with entro-toxemia. We will have to inject if it gets any worse.

Last Thursday I went into Birdwood on the truck for ½ ton pollard to feed the pigs with. It was very cold in the truck with no side curtains.

Yesterday we went to golf and spent a very enjoyable afternoon. My rounds were 59 & 53 & Bruce's were 52 & 63 so you can see we are improving & we like the game very much.

Well Mother I will close. How are Gwenyth's boils they must be painful. Bruce's cold is nearly better. Thank you very much for the pygamas [sic] *toffee, pad & lemons. Hoping my letter will receive your earnest consideration*

Your loving son

Glen

It is a letter which reveals quite a lot about the writer. It's very structured, very formal, the sort of letter children were taught to write at school, and it has been written with great care. Possibly it's a fair copy made after several aborted drafts. It's easy to imagine Glen wondering how best to state his case, chewing his pen, starting to write, rethinking, writing again, scratching out, rewriting. In the end his approach is masterly. He introduces the question, sets out the arguments both for and against, follows this with persuasion. (He was a member of the Scotch College debating society, remember.) Leaving that persuasion to speak for itself, he then abruptly changes tack. He softens, turns his attention to family matters (did his mother receive her Mother's Day gift?) and then lightens the atmosphere with diverting information even further removed from his argument (pigs, lambs, the purchase of pollard). All this is only a decoy. After a few solicitous comments and questions about the family, he delivers the final punch, presented this time in the crisp, no-nonsense language of a business deal.

It's a well-considered letter, and it incorporates a son's understanding of his parents' feelings, but it never wavers in its intent. It's clear that Glen isn't going to change his mind. If his parents refuse him now, he will try again, and again.

Glen was still only eighteen, which was then three years below the age of majority, and predictably his parents were horrified by his request. They could not be unaware of the danger: people said of the air force, with grim jocularity, that it promised the greatest excitement and the quickest death. In the event, knowing the character of their oldest son, they compromised by asking him to wait until he was nineteen. They may have prayed that the war would be over by then, although this time – unlike the First World War – few believed that the conflict in Europe would be of short duration. There was no thought of the dreadful escalation that would happen in December 1941, after Japan's surprise attack on the US fleet at Pearl Harbor.

Glen was not completely starry-eyed about joining the RAAF, nor was he new to military experience. He already knew something of the discipline involved. He had been a sergeant in the Scotch College cadets – a detail entered in his enlistment record. But for now he had no option but to heed his parents' wishes. He would wait. In the meantime, he would learn as much as he could to achieve his other ambition, which was to be a good farmer.

On 4 October 1940, with money lent by their maternal grandmother (and later paid back), the Murrie boys acquired 160 acres of farm land at Eden Valley. This land, Section 543 and part of Section 544, purchased in the name of Mary (Em) Murray and George Murrie, was part of the vast Matthews estate which was now, after years of legal wrangling, being divided up and sold off. The Murries' property was adjacent to a larger portion of the estate (320 acres, comprising Section 542 and part of Section 541), later named Ravenswood, which was bought on the same day in the name of Emily Vigar.[1]

The boys called their property Barunga Park, giving it the name of their grandmother's house, Barunga, in

Knightsbridge. They planned one day to build a house on their property, and to begin farming there. In the meantime, it would be managed by the Vigars.

Chapter 12

Life on the Land

In my memories of them my grandparents were always old – slow, stiff-limbed, grey-haired. My grandfather's hands shook quite badly. I remember, when I was very small, watching in fascination as he tried to eat a piece of fried egg that fell repeatedly from his shaking fork. But in 1940, not as my grandparents, but as Glen's Uncle Will and Aunt Em, they must have been a robust and vigorous pair. He was sixty-one; she was only fifty-seven. To me, now, that seems relatively young, but age was seen differently in the 1940s. Almost from the moment they became mothers, young women turned into matrons. They wore constricting corsets and stockings, even when they were at home. They had their hair permed, and they wouldn't consider going to Town unless they were wearing a hat and gloves. Many, especially rural women, had been fitted with porcelain-white false teeth since their twenties, some even since their teens. Makeup, for those who wore it, consisted of pale orange face powder (a shiny nose was a sign of slatternliness) and red lipstick. My grandmother would never have stooped to wearing makeup: she was what she was, just as God made her.

The war didn't impact hugely on country life. The rhythm of the seasons continued in spite of what was happening overseas. There were still sheep to shear, cows to milk, paddocks to plough, crops to harvest.

Despite his eagerness to leave home, and his enduring interest in cars and mechanics, my father was deeply ingrained with the ways and habits of a farmer. Long after he had sold the paddocks where he learned his trade, he wrote out for me the pattern of a farming year on Avon Brae. Here it is, just as he wrote it. Even now, as I read his scrawled list, I can see his hands, still brown and knobbed and thickened and scarred with decades of farm work, and the wistful light in his eyes as he remembers the eternal round of tasks, once undertaken as a duty, now re-lived with a longing that is partly sentiment, partly a recognition of something deep in the blood, and as familiar and necessary as breath. His writing is scratchy, spiky, sometimes almost illegible.[1]

January

Fruit-picking, especially stone fruit (apricots, plums, nectarines)
Finish off cereal harvest
Hay carting both cereal and grass
Late mating of ewes

February

Grape-picking and carting to wineries
Potatoes to dig

March

Early cultivation for cereal growing (wheat, oats, barley, etc)

Early crops may be fed off to stock to help in tooling out (i.e., more stalks per plant)
Fat stock are sold

April
Firewood to cart in and saw up
Watch for foreign plants which will show up
Pruning of grapes and fruit trees
Superphosphate broadcasting, 90 lbs to the acre

May
Early lambs
Tailing and marking of lambs
Beef cattle are calving for sale in 4 months
Crutching ewes

June (winter)
Make and mend
Watch stock sales to make up any losses on sales earlier
Ploughing

July
Make and mend
Ploughing to finish
Cultivation to finish
Crops to seed

August
Blowflies appear – means a good deal of work
Crutching before shearing for all sheep

September
Shearing, culling for sale after shearing, off shears
Dipping after shearing to control ticks, lice, etc.
Drafting out sale sheep (age & wool) as marked

October
Attending sheep sales in the Lower North for well-grown merino lambs, wethers preferred

November
Start of haymaking or baling clover hay if advanced enough

December
Cereal hay to be cut early
Apricots to be cut & dried. Cherries ditto
Irrigation to be attended to and modified

All through the year
Rabbit control, fencing to maintain, machinery to maintain, cows to milk, chooks to feed

This was the world into which Glen and Bruce were now plunged. The work was often hard, but they would have found most of it novel and interesting, even exciting. I'm sure my kind-hearted grandfather would have introduced them fairly gradually to their new regime, but still it must have seemed, at first, unrelenting.

The world of the farmer is a world spent mostly out of doors. It can be unbearably hot in summer, muddy and freezing in winter. It is a world of aching muscles and sunburn, of cuts and bruises, of sun-dazzled eyes, wool boils, dust-clogged noses and woollen socks prickly with grass-seeds. It is a world constantly threatened by drought, bushfire, and diseases of animals and crops. It is tough, dirty, messy and often unpredictable, but at the same time it is beautiful in its simplicity. It is life at its most fundamental: a world of birth and death, of growth and decay, of unceasing labour and uncertain reward. Nothing can soften its uncompromising reality.

One of my most treasured possessions is a small, shabby pocket notebook that belonged to my great-grandfather William Matthews Vigar and is still marked by his earthy fingerprints. Amid the painstaking records of purchases and deals, rainfall, harvest yields, details of piglets and foals and lambs born and lost, is the entry for 28 August 1896: *25 Minutes to 10 o'clock My Dear Wife Susannah Vigar Died.* The little notebook, a modest but invaluable record of a farming life, was passed down to my grandfather Will, who wrote in his turn: *Father died on May 28/01 at a quarter past three o'clock in the afternoon very suddenly.*

In 1901 my grandfather was twenty-two years old; now he was an orphan. Susannah was his stepmother, his father's second wife. His own mother, Jane, had died when he was only nine – a photograph of the family in mourning shows him as a thin, big-eyed, serious-faced little boy – and the unexpected loss of the father for whom he was named would have hit him hard. The notebook entries are no less heartfelt for their brevity.

Beneath the lines recording his father's death, Will has written in pencil, in childishly unformed handwriting: *My Motto. I know that the Lord will give you all that is good for you, if you fear him and do your best.* Less than two weeks later he writes *Wheat sown by me in Eden Vally [*sic*] Paddocks. Commenced drilling 8 June 1901. Started with Darks Improved on main road side.* Following this are details for drilling and sowing *Purple Straw, White Tuscan, Brown Tuscan, Fox Tail Oats, Californian* and *Field Peas* (in total, 1544 acres under crop). And, on 3 August, *Flora calved.*

In farming there can be little room for sentiment.

Forty years later, Glen and Bruce learned from their now elderly Uncle Will the basics of farm management. They learned to milk a cow, to plough and harrow, to aid a farrowing sow, to kill a sheep for the table. In his methodical way, my grandfather would have made sure his pupils were properly trained, that they could recognise the difference between good and inferior wheat seed, judge the quality and ply of a fleece, diagnose and medicate foot rot and scabby mouth and scouring. They would have learned how to crutch flyblown sheep, how to dip them to prevent infestations of ticks and lice, how to tail a lamb, what to do when a sheep is 'down'.

Milking was one of their constant and most important jobs. Every morning and every evening, with the help of Laurel, the Vigars' live-in maid, Glen and Bruce milked the cows by hand. As more cows were added to the small herd, the job became increasingly time-consuming. Bruce recalls that there was great excitement when at last Uncle Will bought an Alfa-Laval milking machine – not that it made getting up at crack of dawn on frosty mornings any easier.

In September, the most important month in the sheep-farmer's year, the jackeroos took part in shearing, acting as rouseabouts in the shed, helping on the skirting table and the wool press, even tentatively having a go at shearing.

The atmosphere at shearing time is one of constant busyness and importance. With any luck the spring weather will be fine: rain can disrupt proceedings for many days, as it's impossible to shear a wet sheep. The dandelions turn the paddocks to gold, and the sun shines, and there is constant noise: the hubbub of shouting to be heard above the pulsating roar of the shearing machines, the ruckus of solid woolly sheep jostling for position, their hoofs clattering on the slatted wooden floor of the holding pens, the determined barking of sheepdogs, the dust, the pungent, all-pervading smell of greasy wool. And the clunk of the doors beside each shearing stand as each newly shorn sheep, thin, white, ridged, spotted with blood, is pushed out to join its strangely denuded fellows.

Then there is the sudden silence for smoko, and the lighting of roll-your-own cigarettes, and the pouring of black tea and consumption of biscuits brought down from the house, and in the silence the sound of blowflies can be heard, and the constant tremulous baa-ing of the penned animals still awaiting the terrifying buzzing shears.

When it is shearing time at Avon Brae the old wooden shearing shed is the centre of the universe. Everyone is part of a team, from the women preparing food in the homestead kitchen to the tall city boys who lend a hand wherever it's needed – sweeping the oily floor, rolling up the fleeces, working the wool press. There isn't much time for contemplation. Slowly the pile of rock-hard bales stencilled in black with the name AVON BRAE grows bigger.

Glen and Bruce worked hard and with great enthusiasm.

It wasn't in their nature to do otherwise, and the simple, down-to-earth farming lifestyle suited them perfectly. And they weren't without diversions and entertainment. There were movies ('a Benbow Amusements Show') every weekend in the Mount Pleasant Institute, and there was a constant stream of hospitality, for this was a time when most country families knew each other well and quite often were related. (Many of those picture cards at the head of big families in the area were siblings, or first cousins, or relatives by marriage.) There were also social gatherings connected with the church – bun nights, card evenings, fetes. Uncle Will and Aunt Em were stalwart supporters of Eden Valley's Congregational church. The number of young men was dwindling as more and more enlisted, but dances, often in support of charities, were still held at nearby Keyneton and elsewhere, and local sporting clubs were eager to make use of the Murrie brothers' abilities. Glen had no great interest in football, but he played a decent game of cricket and (as we have seen) he was a good golfer. He also played tennis, and the old Wolseley would often have taken him and Bruce to tennis parties around the district. On their days off the boys were as free as birds – provided they were back at the farm in time for the evening milking.

And all the time the war raged overseas.

Chapter 13

Nineteen

This letter, from Glen to his father, is dated 20 February 1941. It is written from Avon Brae.

Dear Dad, it begins.

It has [been] fairly hot up here today and we are all feeling fairly tired tonight. We have been pretty busy what with feeding the cattle & carting wood & stones etc. Please excuse this writing Dad as I am sitting in an easy chair.

Well Dad I got my car on Tuesday from the mechanic and it is running perfectly. It is very easy to start now, only requiring one turn of the handle to start it.

Dad I want to thank you for letting me enlist in the R.A.A.F. – you don't know how much I have wanted to join & what it means to me. I have prayed about it since last year and I feel that I am doing the right thing. Mr Gratton [Norm Gratton, the headmaster at Scotch College] sent me a wonderful reference & a nice note of good luck, also Mr Mellor. Have you seen Mr Webster, Dad? also have you sent Mr Hughes his letter.

Today we dipped about a case of plums in caustic soda and put them on a tray to dry. They should be very nice.

Well Dad I expect Mother will tell you all the news so I will close, hoping to see you on [the] 7th

Love from Glen
P.S. Bruce said would you mind getting pamphlet 198 from the Dept. of Ag. Glen.

The '7th' Glen refers to is 7 March, his nineteenth birthday. Seeing his parents is not the only thing he has planned for that day. He is also driving to Adelaide, accompanied by Bruce, to enlist in the RAAF. He may not be old enough to vote, but he is old enough to put his life on the line for his country.

He enrols at No. 5 Recruiting Centre. His physical development is described as 'Good'. His hearing and vision are perfect, his colour vision normal. His Complexion is Medium; Eyes Brown; Hair Dark Brown. He is six feet and half an inch tall, and weighs 155 pounds. His chest measures 35 inches. He has two scars, one on his third right-hand finger, and one at his hairline. His religious denomination is Baptist. He has been convicted of a single Traffic Offence. He gives his previous trade or profession as Sheep Farming.

He signs his name, solemnly and sincerely affirming and declaring that he will well and truly serve 'Our Sovereign Lord the King' as a member of the Air Force Reserve of the Commonwealth of Australia, and that he will resist His Majesty's enemies and cause His Majesty's Peace to be kept and maintained. For Glen this is far more than lip service.

From now on he will be known officially by his Service Number, 416600.

A manila envelope in Glen's service file contains his passport-sized photograph. He looks fresh, hopeful, and extraordinarily young. It is the likeness of someone who knows he is at the very beginning of life's adventure, and is absolutely certain that it will be good.[1]

And what of his birthday tea, in Hazelwood Park? It seems likely that the whole family would have been there. As it was a Friday, David may have managed to wangle an early weekend away from Roseworthy, and Gwenyth, now almost twelve, would be home from school. Lulu would have made a birthday cake – an iced fruit cake, stuck with nineteen candles; and there would be other edible treats, as well as gifts from everyone. But one can only imagine the thoughts swirling in George and Lulu's minds as they gazed fondly at their oldest son and tried to suppress their fears.

Glen's attestation was filled out, again at No. 5 Recruiting Centre, on 21 July 1941. As an Aircraftman Class 2, the lowest rank, he was appointed to No. 4 Initial Training School at Mount Breckan in Victor Harbor, one of four such schools opened in Australia under the auspices of the Empire Air Training Scheme.[2]

Mount Breckan, originally built in 1881 and still a south coast landmark, was a gothic-style mansion high on a hill overlooking the sea. It had thirty-eight rooms, two cellars, a five-storey tower and a golf course.[3] There would be no flying lessons here, but Glen would be assessed for his suitability to take up a role in the RAAF, either as a pilot or as a navigator, wireless operator or air gunner. Here, with dozens of other new recruits, he would learn the basics of air force life – drill, marching and physical training. He would also be taught fundamental skills including maths and physics, navigation, aerodynamics, armaments and ship recognition, Morse code,

Glen, on leave from Mount Breckan, with Bruce, Gwenyth and David at Eden Valley

and the Rules of the Air. The course ran for eight weeks for potential air gunners and twelve weeks for 'air observers' (air crew trained in reconnaissance). For those who were seen as having the ability to become pilots, the acknowledged elite, the course would be extended to fourteen weeks.

With its intensive program of lessons combined with highly regimented communal living, Mount Breckan was a bit like boarding school, but boarding school with regular inspections and parades. There were new people to meet and befriend, new rules to learn, and new clothes – everything from singlets to boots. On top of this there were what might have seemed like unexpected gifts: a neat sewing kit known as a 'housewife', a boot-cleaning kit, razors, a mess tin, cutlery, blankets and towels. All of it free! Everything had to be stashed neatly in a kitbag – also new.

The sense of newness permeated everything. The dusty boots, out-of-elbow jumpers and stained work trousers of the hard-working jackeroo were replaced by the faint chemical smell of smooth, unworn fabric, precise, razor-sharp folds, the squeak of new boots. Regulation uniform consisted of blue overalls and a pullover in cold weather, khaki shorts and shirt in summer. A field service cap with a white flash indicated each recruit's status as an air crew trainee.

Trainees were housed in tents, but classes were held in the draughty, high-ceilinged rooms of the mansion itself. For Glen, life in this unusual setting must have been strange enough. The strangeness would have been compounded by the realisation that he was in uniform, in training for war service, at a place very close to the beach where he had spent so many sunny holidays with his family. Lazing on the sand at Port Elliot, queuing for Dandy ice creams at the kiosk, fishing off the jetty – all these childhood memories were now dreamlike, part of another age.

The final allocation of positions in the RAAF depended not only on the recruit's physical and mental ability, but on the numbers of pilots, navigators or gunners required at the time. To his great relief and delight, Glen was selected to train as a pilot. Promoted to Leading Aircraftman, he was posted on 15 October to Western Junction, No. 7 Elementary Flying Training School (EFTS), near Launceston in Tasmania. There were now twelve such training schools throughout the country. He would be at Western Junction for three months.

Chapter 14

Western Junction

Glen began his Elementary Training Course (Pilot) on 19 October 1941, and recorded his progress formally in the logbook he maintained – as all pilots must – throughout his flying career. He also wrote a less formal account, in the form of a personal diary, in a small notebook. On the first page of this notebook he has written, as a schoolboy might,

416600 MURRIE G.I.
FLIGHING DAIRY.
R.A.A.F.

Glen's first experience of flying, like that of all the trainees, was a familiarisation flight in a DH82 Tiger Moth. The little Tiger biplanes looked like toy planes made of wood and string, but they were used in training because they were easy to fly and very forgiving of novice pilots' mistakes. They had two cockpits, one behind the other, each one fully instrumented so that either the instructor or the student could take control.[1]

The day for which the first flight was scheduled was a huge disappointment. Glen's first diary entry reads:

We were going up for first flight today but the weather is terrible, wet, with 40 mph gale blowing. Met our flighing

instructors who gave us cockpit & parachute drill. Our instructor, F.O. Scasgilini [the name is in slightly smaller handwriting, and has apparently been added later], is a fine chap and gives one complete confidence in himself.[2]

So, no flying yet. The next entry, for 20 October, describes Glen's initial experience. Although he puts a brave face on it, it was not quite what he expected:

Had my first flight today and first dual. Managed fairly well but plane seems possessed sometimes. Was very sick but soon felt OK again. We climbed to 4000 [feet] to get over rough stuff but got tossed all over the sky so descended. I am looking forward to a good hour's flying tomorrow. Got in 15 mins dual.

It was not an easy introduction to what he had wanted to do for much of his life, but if he had any misgivings, Glen refused to succumb to them.

His second day in the air was an improvement on the first.

Took off at 7 o'clock, beautiful day on ground but very rough at 2000 ft. Took over at 1500 and climbed to 8500 where it was comparatively calm. Practised straight & level flying, then did four gliding stalls & then one power stall. Then started gliding. Followed instructor through in landing. Felt a lot better today although stalls made my stomach rise a bit. Got 45 mins in today. Did a little propeller swinging and starting drill. Hope to start gliding turns and approaches tomorrow. Also did taxying today.

The next day was better still.

Beautiful day on the ground today but rough up top again. Took off @ 1000 hrs and climbed by myself to 3000 ft. Flew over Launceston & then headed back still climbing. Practised medium turns and gliding turns which are pretty tough. The instructor gave me my first loop today and are they good? I landed her myself today & made quite a good job of it although he talked me into the fields. Have now got 1 hr 50 mins dual up.

Already he is beginning to think like a pilot, referring to the plane as 'her', describing bad weather as 'rough up top'. His boyish excitement at doing his first loop shines through his writing, but typically he remains focused and level-headed.

The weather continued to be poor, and flying was 'scrubbed' for a day, after which, on 24 October, Glen reports that he flew from 0600 hrs to 0700 hrs. His confidence is increasing:

For the first time it was as calm as a mill pond and enjoyed every minute in the air. Concentrated on circuits with landings and take-offs. Can manage the landings fairly well but career all over the 'drome in the take-offs but practice will improve them. I landed two fairly good ones and ballooned the third, but made up for it on the last one which was a beauty.

With fine weather, and his queasiness largely conquered, Glen is beginning to feel at home in the air. He is also beginning to feel modestly proud of his achievements so far. He has the maturity to look at those achievements objectively – to assess what he has done well, and pinpoint what he could do better. Nothing short of excellence will do.

What are his feelings now, as he goes up in the little Tiger Moth? Wonder, undoubtedly, as he gazes down at the rolling green countryside far below him. Wonder, as he sees what the world looks like from a great height: Liliputian buildings, newly shorn sheep like grains of rice, the silver thread of the River Tamar, tiny cars on pencilled roads. Mingled with wonder is elation, the sort of joy he felt when he helped row his school to victory just two-and-a-half years earlier. And almost certainly a sense of great freedom as he peers out at the limitless blue of the sky.

The tiny plane in which he is sitting shakes and rattles. The wind whistles through the wing struts. Glen knows his life depends on something seemingly as fragile as a box kite with an engine, yet he has no fear of falling to earth. The air is an element he inhabits perfectly, as a bird does.

He can't wait to fly solo.

Three days later Glen writes that he has 'got the hang of taking off', and did the last circuit all by himself. 'The instructor told me today that I should be off solo in the required 7 hours minimum, so feel quite bucked up.' And next day, 'F.O. Scasgilini told me today that I was ready to go solo after today's lesson, but would have to [wait] until I reached the minimum of 7 hours which is a nark.'

In the end, though, the rule was waived.

Western Junction, 31.10.41. Went up this morning for 3 circuits and landings and then F.O. Maloney took me up for my solo test. I made two perfect circuits and landings and after I landed the second time he got out, took out the 'stick and sent me up by myself, and what a thrill it was to be the first pilot of a Tiger Moth. It took me four circuits to get her down and [I] brought her in the fourth time on 3 points. I was the first of our lot to go solo without any previous flying experience so didn't do so badly, getting off in 6 hours 40 minutes.

After that it was all practice: climbing turns, gliding turns, steep turns, medium turns, side slips, circuits and landings, instrument flying ('you've certainly got to trust those instruments'), powered approaches ('Have got steep turns taped now, but powered approaches have me worried now but they will come'). Far too often flying was 'scrubbed' because of 'boisterous weather conditions up top'. On 4 November Glen wrote that he did a spin solo: 'I climbed to 6000 ft to do it and came out after 500 ft drop which was not so bad. The first solo spin certainly takes some doing, but after the first spin you want to do

An early photo of Glen, probably taken during his first weeks of pilot training

more.' By 8 November, having done 'everything possible in a Tiger Moth', he thinks he has finally conquered the airsickness that plagued him earlier during aerobatic manoeuvres.

As the days pass he does more aerobatics, and finds them thrilling, although slow rolls are a difficulty. He also does some low flying and 'shot up a couple of houses ... Low flying is extra good'. One of his fellow students spins his plane off a gliding turn and crashes, escaping serious injury but leaving the plane a 'complete wipe-off ... I expect there was about £1200 worth damage'. A day later another trainee 'stood a Tiger on her nose in the centre of the 'drome, smashed a prop. & wing tip and 'cart but got out unhurt'.

Glen himself doesn't escape trouble. He is, after all, still a teenager. On 13 November 'I got put on the map for ground looping in the centre of the drome. I had to climb the "golden stairs" to the duty pilot's tower'.

Two days later 'Our instructor picked a couple of dog fights and did we have a time, it was the greatest thrill of my life, twisting, turning, rolling and in general, had a wonderful time'.

His first night flight, on 19 November, was exciting in a different way:

Wind dropped down towards evening tonight and night flying was organised. I was not up until 11.35 pm and it was beautiful up, there was not a bump in the sky. We did 5 circuits and landings and [I] was getting the feel of them by midnight when we finished. The 'drome looked beautiful lit up from the air just like Luna Park.

He continues to practise, seizing any hours he can. The boy who doggedly worked at perfecting his rowing technique applies the same sort of dedication to his flying. When conditions are rough, he practises forced landings, powered approaches and powered landings, cross-wind take-offs and landings. On one occasion 'we made the old Tiger fly backwards the wind was so strong'. Cold, windy Tasmania was living up to its reputation.

'By the time we have finished at this station,' Glen later comments wryly, 'we should be able to fly in any weather. Now have 25 hrs 30 mins up.'

On 22 November he records that 'I have now finished the syllabus & all I need now is tons of practice'. But it isn't easy to practise when the weather is so unpredictable. 'If we don't get some good weather soon,' he notes on 25 November, 'we shall be flying all day and night. Some have 20 hours to get up in 14 days and already all leave has been cancelled.'

He still has 'a good lot of trouble' with slow rolls, but believes that he is 'getting the feel of them now'.

On 27 November, during a period of dual instruction, he learns how to do a roll off the top of a loop, 'and they are extra good & not so hard as a slow roll . . . I did some acrobats over the drome at 6000 ft for the instructor to see and made a howling mess of a slow roll & came out upside down in a dive at 140 M.P.H. Those Tigers can certainly stand a good hammering'.

The next day he does his instrument test, and passes 'above average'.

On 6 December (and you can sense the pang of regret) Glen has his 'last training flip in a Tiger Moth'.

On 7 December he goes to Hobart for two days of leave.

It's a date to remember. On 7 December 1941 the American Naval Base at Pearl Harbor was attacked, with no warning, by fighter planes of the Imperial Japanese Navy. The possibility of fighting in the skies over Europe – the aim of all Australian trainee pilots – receded. Suddenly Australia itself was on the front line.

When Glen returned to the station on 9 December he was astonished by what he saw. 'I found the place in a state of chaos with planes picketed everywhere & everyone digging trenches & filling sandbags.'

It was the end of his time at Western Junction. After a talk with his Flying Instructor and Commanding Officer he found that he had 'managed to get "Above Average" for flying & a good report on other work'. He was far too modest. On his final summary, in the section headed ANY POINTS IN FLYING OR AIRMANSHIP WHICH SHOULD BE WATCHED, Glen's Commanding Officer had written: 'A pupil pilot possessing outstanding ability.'

Glen now had a grand total of 51 hours and 25 minutes' flying experience, with 25.05 hours as pilot.

Two days later, on 11 December, he was told that he was being posted to No. 7 Service Flying Training School (SFTS) at Deniliquin, in the Riverina district of New South Wales. Here he would take the Advanced Training Course in operational or service flying, beginning his instruction with the Intermediate Training Squadron.

On the same day Germany and Italy declared war on the United States, and the United States reciprocated. The world was now plunged into all-out war.

Chapter 15

Flying Solo

The course at No. 7 SFTS lasted for sixteen weeks and included the following 'Sequence of Instruction':

1. *Familiarity with cockpit layout*
2. *Air experience*
3. *Taxiing (including handling of engine)*
4. *Straight and level flying*
5. *Climbing and gliding*
6. *Stalling (with incipient spin)*
7. *Medium turns*
8. *Climbing turns*
9. *Taking-off into wind*
10. *Powered approach and landing*
11. *Going around again*
12. *Gliding approach and landing*
13. *Action in event of fire*
14. *Abandoning the aircraft*
15. *Forced landings (elementary)*
16. *First solo*
17. *Instrument flying*
18. *Taking-off and landing with varying degrees of flap*
19. *Low flying (with instructor only)*
20. *Precautionary landings*
21. *Steep turns*
22. *Spinning (with engine on and off)*
23. *Aerobatics*

24. *Forced landings (advanced)*
25. *Navigation*
26. *Formation*
27. *Night flying*[1]

Some of these skills ('Familiarity with cockpit layout', 'Straight and level flying') seem quite basic. Others ('Action in event of fire', 'Abandoning the aircraft', 'Forced landings') would have brought home forcibly to trainees the realisation that flying, and especially flying in battle, contained more than an element of danger. Only the most laidback of student pilots, only the least imaginative, could have ignored the sombre implication of these aspects of the course.

Training was given on Wirraways, which were considered ideal trainer aircraft because they had most of the characteristics of the fighter aircraft in use at the time. The Wirraway (the name is an Aboriginal word meaning 'challenge') was generally known as 'the pilot maker'. A single-engined general purpose plane armed with two forward-facing Vickers .303 machine-guns, it was made in Australia under licence by the Commonwealth Aircraft Corporation.[2]

Glen began the SFTS course on 15 December 1941, after a short period of leave. Four days later, after only seven hours of dual instruction, he flew solo. On 7 March 1942, his twentieth birthday, he was awarded his Flying Badge or 'Wings', the insignia of the qualified pilot – an achievement in which he must have taken a great deal of quiet pride. Shortly afterwards, as listed in his logbook, he began instruction in 'low level bombing'; a month later the duty listed was 'high dive bombing'.

By the time he completed the Advanced course, on

Glen at Wandeen in 1942, shortly after receiving his Wings. He still wears the cap with the white flash indicating trainee status

22 April, Glen had flown for a grand total of 147 hours and 35 minutes. As a pilot he was assessed, again, as 'above average', but in bombing he achieved only an 'average' rating and in air gunnery 'below average (inexperienced)'.

Meanwhile the war in the Pacific had been gathering momentum. On 15 February 1942, in what is still seen as the worst defeat ever suffered by the British Army, the British colony of Singapore fell to the Japanese. From then on, the Japanese advance seemed unstoppable. Indo-China, Malaya and the Philippines had been invaded. Thousands of Australian servicemen were killed or captured as they tried to hold a defensive line stretching from Malaya in the west to New Guinea in the east. With most of the RAAF squadrons fighting in Europe and North Africa, resources were stretched to breaking point, and the Australian, British, American and Dutch forces in the Pacific were overwhelmed. Many Allied servicemen were captured by the Japanese and taken as prisoners of war. Australia was becoming increasingly isolated and vulnerable.[3]

In fact Australia had already been invaded, although most Australians knew little about it. On 19 February, just days after the fall of Singapore, Darwin had suffered two disastrous Japanese air raids. The official Government position was that only seventeen people had been killed. The real toll, which was not made known until decades later, was much worse: at least 243 people dead, and between 300 and 400 wounded. Eight ships at anchor in the harbour, including the destroyer USS *Peary*, were sunk, and twenty war planes were destroyed. Most of Darwin's civil and military facilities were wiped out.

It now seems inconceivable that most of this information was deliberately kept from the Australian public, but it was done, however misguidedly, in the interests of maintaining morale. As late as 30 April the *Grenfell Record* published this falsely reassuring article:

JAP INVASION 'Not Likely Now,' Says Press Writer.

According to a special representative of the 'Courier-Mail', who has been touring the 'springboard' in the north, the Jap is in for some surprises if he attempts to invade Australia. He adds: – Back of Moresby, in North Queensland, wonders have been worked in preparing a North Australian defence line which may become the attack line for MacArthur's offensive against the Japanese. Allied troops have been rushed north, equipment has been sent, fixed defences have sprung up overnight, and – greatest factor of all – fighter and bomber planes have been massing. These things have bred confidence among the troops, and that feeling of assurance has spread through the community in North Queensland . . . The Japanese now have no easy prospect of establishing themselves on the Australian mainland, if they have any prospect at all. Short of an invasion the Japanese may try nuisance bombing raids anywhere along the coast. Value of these is questionable because Allied bombers will not take long to seek out and attack any enemy aircraft carrier off the Australian coast.

On 24 May 1942, three months after the horrific events at Darwin, and quite unaware of their scale, Bruce Murrie drove to Port Adelaide. Here, aged only eighteen, he enlisted as an Ordinary Seaman in the Royal Australian Naval Reserve. He rose swiftly through the ranks, becoming a Midshipman only six months later, on 9 November 1942. By the war's end he would be a Lieutenant.

David was still studying at Roseworthy. Soon he too

The Murrie family after Bruce's enlistment. Glen and Gwenyth are standing; in front of them (from left) are David, George Murrie, Lulu Murrie, and Bruce

would enlist, choosing to join the RAAF, like his older brother. By the start of 1943 George and Lulu were to have three sons in uniform.

After completing their course at the SFTS, most pilots could expect to be posted to an Operational Training Unit (OTU), where they would train on aircraft used in war zones. Glen could have been posted to an OTU like the one at Mildura, where pilots converted to Kittyhawks or Spitfires. However, after brief postings to Station Headquarters, Laverton (from 11 May) and the General Reconnaissance School at Cressy (from 25 May) he was sent, on 30 May 1942, to the New South Wales town of Parkes for further training.

RAAF Station Parkes, formed in 1941 as part of the Empire Air Training Scheme, was home to several units, including No. 1 Air Navigation School, No. 2 Wireless Air Gunners School, No. 8 Operational Training Unit and the Central Flying School.[4] Given his proven ability, Glen may have feared that he would be given the task of becoming an instructor – an occasionally nerve-racking job reserved for pilots who showed responsibility and talent above the norm. No doubt to his relief, that didn't happen.

In comparative terms the Air Navigation School course was a long one, lasting from May 1942 to the end of the year. During this time, as recorded in his logbook, Glen flew Avro Ansons, Wirraways, CAC (Commonwealth Aircraft Corporation) Wackett Trainers, Moth Minors and DH89 Dragon Rapides. On 29 June, with effect from 30 April, he was promoted to the rank of Pilot Officer.

As a pilot who was eager to serve his country, Glen may initially have been disappointed by his posting to Parkes because it kept him far from the action overseas. However, as this door closed, another opened, and it was to bring him rewards of an entirely different kind.

Chapter 16

Nancy

The events that would bring Glen and Nancy together were moving inexorably to their conclusion. Like my father, Glen was to meet his future fiancée at a dance.

By 1942 Nancy Priddle had grown into an attractive young woman, dark-haired, blue-eyed, and with a ready smile. She had finished her education at Kambala, an Anglican private school for girls in Sydney's Rose Bay, and she was now working in local government at Forbes as a clerk for Jemalong Shire. (Later she would be promoted to assistant Shire Clerk.) As someone who loved being with people, Nancy enjoyed her job well enough, but it wasn't for her the start of a career trajectory. To all intents and purposes she was doing what so many young women did then: marking time before marriage.

Nancy was a romantic. She believed, utterly, in love, and had seen the happy outcome of a romance in her own family, in April, when her sister June had married Vic Bradford. It was a quiet wedding, as Vic was on leave from active service with the AIF in New Guinea, but Nancy had revelled in the preparations, simple though they were – the frock, the cake, the flowers for the church (which was reported in the *Grenfell Record* as 'very tastefully decorated').[1] She was sure that she too would fall in love, and the man she fell in love with would become her husband. He was out there somewhere, waiting for her. In the meantime, her life was a pleasantly repetitive round of paid employment, domestic work and social outings – church, tennis, dances, parties.

Being part of a large, friendly community allowed country people of all ages many opportunities to get together, and there were few activities more entertaining than an organised dance. A ball promised so much on so many levels: good companionship, healthy exercise, excellent and copious refreshments (although in general there was officially no alcohol) and, for the younger set, the teasing possibility of a new or continuing romance.

The appointment of a dance committee, the allocation of roles, and the preparation of the chosen venue allowed for weeks of pleasurable activity. Apart from that, for many women there was the private enjoyment of planning and sewing a new ball gown, or transforming an old one. The war had imposed a number of stringencies, among them restrictions on fabric and clothing, but there was a great deal a clever needlewoman could do to freshen up outdated finery.

The main disadvantage to holding a ball was the relative imbalance of women, as many of the district's young men had joined up and were either fighting overseas or in training camps around the country.

Nancy and her family were enthusiastic supporters both of dances and of the newly established branch of the Red Cross at Grenfell. When the branch decided to hold a ball in aid of the Prisoners of War Fund, and settled on the night of 27 August, Nancy would have looked forward to it with the fresh openness and enthusiasm with which she entered into every social activity, regardless of what 'possibilities' it might offer. Perhaps, like many single girls, she wondered if she might meet an interesting man on this particular night, but her main objective would have been simply to have fun. The ball may well have been a family affair: her parents would be likely to support such a worthy cause. Her married sister June may also have been there, and her oldest sister, Lorraine.

The subsequent description of the ball published in the *Grenfell Record* on 1 September 1942 might seem to modern readers a little quaint in its self-consciously inflated style, but beneath the pomposity there is much cheeriness and kindly goodwill.

The Oddfellows' Hall was comfortably filled on the evening of Thursday last when the first ball conducted by the local branch of the Red Cross Society was held.

The success of the function justified the optimism and enterprise of the promoters who are to be congratulated on giving public proof that, after an entertainment of this character, patrons can aver that nothing has offended, and everything has pleased, their susceptibilities.

Branch officials met the Mayor (Ald Livingstone) and Mayoress on arrival, and a handsome posy was gracefully accepted by Mrs. Livingstone.

Shortly afterwards the Branch President, Mrs. W. Douglass, and Hon. Secretary, Mr. F. A. V. Rochfort, escorted the Mayoral party to the stage, where Mr. Rochfort, on behalf of the committee, extended a warm welcome to Mr. and Mrs. Livingstone. He said that sentiment was extended to the many patrons who graced the floor that evening. He would not inflict a lengthy delivery on his auditors, and after sincerely thanking them for their attendance, asked their own enthusiastic President to accept, from her fellow workers, a magnificent bouquet which Mrs. G. W. Simpson then presented. The speaker concluded by stating that sufficient cash donations and incidental receipts were in hand to more than cover ball expenses so that the entire proceeds would be available for the advertised purpose, the Prisoners of War Fund. The Mayor stated that he gratefully accepted the courtesies of the branch and was particularly happy to be present, with his wife, to officially open the ball. The Red Cross Society was doing a noble and charitable work, essentially patriotic in character; its objects were to solely assist war victims and prisoners who could not help themselves. With all the sincerity at his command he appealed to all to extend to the society, and the local branch in particular, that degree of support which would further stimulate their zeal.

The Grenfell branch was only in its infancy, and he could assure the officials that they could expect a full measure of co-operation from the general public. The large attendance could be accepted not only as a tribute to the society, and its objectives, but as a very definite vote of confidence in their branch officials. (The hon. secretary, "Thank you, Mr. Mayor"). He concluded by wishing the society every success, and assuring it of his full support. (Applause). Dancing was immediately in full swing. The floor, prepared by Mr. Bensley, was in excellent order, and the music provided by the youthful "Ace" Orchestra, of Cowra, was of a particularly high calibre. The several extras also suffered nothing by comparison.

The chaste floral stage decorations were effected by Mrs. J. A. Davidson's team who very obviously had 'been at the game before.' Supper of traditional Grenfell excellence was served in three relays, and the ladies are to be warmly commended on their selection and dispensation of a varied and tasty menu. Visitors including military and R.A.A.F. rankings were present from as far afield as Temora and Parkes, and it was almost 3 a.m. when the National Anthem concluded a function, the conduct of which added cubits to the prestige of the branch . . .

The dancing hasn't started yet. All eyes are still on the stage, occupied by well-scrubbed middle-aged men in dinner suits, some with old-fashioned wing collars. Next to them, seated in a row, are their wives, hair freshly permed, silk or brocade dresses garlanded with fur stoles (mostly marmot or lapin, but the Mayoress, still holding her handsome posy, may be wearing a coveted mink). On each side of the official guests are the floral decorations: nothing too spectacular this time, because it has been a particularly cold winter and the spring flowers have been late to bloom, but the ladies have done their best, with white blossom and greenery predominating. On the floor, younger people wait impatiently for the Mayor to stop talking so they can get on with the dancing.

The hall isn't crowded, but it is, as the *Record*'s writer has noted, comfortably filled. The turnout is less than hoped for because the night is unseasonably chilly, and also because since the war there has been a constant demand on the public purse. The Red Cross is just one charity asking for support, and people are beginning to feel the pinch.

The Ace Orchestra strikes up. The first dancers take to the floor: married or engaged couples, official guests. Brothers and sisters dance, cousins and friends and neighbours. Many are dancing partners of long standing. But there are strangers among the crowd, too. Some, hopeful for pleasant diversion and even a little light dalliance, have travelled a considerable distance to get to the Oddfellows' Hall – from outlying farms and small townships, from larger towns like Parkes and Cowra and Temora, Young and West Wyalong. Of these strangers, by far the most interesting to the unattached women are the young servicemen. They stand in a group at one side of the hall, laughing, egging each other on to make the first move. Many are city men, unused to country ways: to them the Red Cross Ball may seem very unsophisticated compared with similar events in Sydney or Melbourne or Brisbane, although they have been told that the refreshments will make the journey worthwhile. Perhaps they have smiled a little, tongue in cheek, at the ponderous formality of proceedings up until this moment.

The RAAF group particularly stand out from the rest. Many of the older local farmers and businessmen have come in correct evening dress, some of the younger or less affluent have had to make do with 'best' suits, but all of them, consciously or subconsciously, will feel overshadowed by the uniformed servicemen. A few, as a consequence, will become loud and silly by way of compensation. Some, to the annoyance of their female relatives, will from time to time exit the hall and sit outside in the bitter cold, passing around a comforting hip flask.

The attraction to women of a man in military uniform is well documented. It has been an undisputed fact ever since

A formal portrait of Glen in uniform

the younger Bennet girls declared their overwhelming partiality for redcoats in *Pride and Prejudice* – and probably long before that. The attendance of the military at the Red Cross Ball would have brightened proceedings considerably for a number of women, and many would have hoped they might be singled out for a dance or two. There was nothing a girl could do about that, of course, but sit, rearrange her skirts, primp her hair, look pleasant, and hope that the young man in the blue RAAF uniform now crossing the shining floor might be making a beeline for her, and not the equally hopeful girl sitting next to her.

Does Nancy notice Glen straight away? He has already attracted covert female attention. He is taller than most: lean, dark, good-looking. His photographs show that he has an engaging smile and nice teeth (nice natural teeth are a rarity in those days of poor dental hygiene and basic dentistry, so they are worthy of note). As he walks towards her, Nancy must see that smile, and it may catch at her heart, just a little.

And what does Glen see? Nancy loves to dance, and for this evening she has made a special effort to look attractive. She is wearing her prettiest evening frock – I imagine something in rose-coloured silk taffeta – and her dancing shoes. She has put on jewellery, too: perhaps a string of pearls, perhaps a necklace in the newly fashionable sparkly marcasite. Her dark hair has been meticulously waved, and her lipstick matches her dress. Up close she smells deliciously of face powder and some flowery perfume. But more than any of these things, Glen notices her eyes, clear and blue, and the sweetness, the *friendliness*, of her expression. He hadn't been sure whether he wanted to make the sixty-mile trip out to Grenfell on such a cold evening, but his colleagues managed to persuade him that he worked too hard and needed some time off. Now, looking at Nancy, and even before he has spoken to her, he's glad they did.

Sometimes it happens that two people meet and feel immediately as if they have been waiting for each other all their lives. There is an instant sense of familiarity and connection. Coupled with this is a powerful attraction, a sense of suddenly entering an unknown world, but a world that promises ever-extending horizons of excitement and discovery.

From the moment Glen says, 'May I have this dance?', from the moment of Nancy's acceptance, from the moment their hands touch for the first time, it's as if they have known each other for ever.

And why not? They are both young and attractive. In spite of his many achievements, Glen is not yet twenty-one. Nancy has just had her nineteenth birthday. They have a great deal in common, especially a love of the land, and their family backgrounds are remarkably similar. Nancy, with her bubbly personality, quickly draws out the quieter Glen: they are perfect foils for each other. With Nancy, Glen feels comfortable, somehow more confident. With Glen, Nancy feels older, even a little protective, but she is also slightly in awe of him. This is in part the romance of the uniform, but it is also respect for a man who has the courage and the skill to be a pilot and fight for his country. Nancy has never been on a plane, and to actually fly one seems to her an amazingly brave and difficult thing to do.

They talk and talk. Glen is entranced by Nancy's femininity. In many respects his life has been male-dominated.

The oldest of three brothers, he has gone to all-male schools, and then worked as a jackeroo with his brother, and then joined the air force with, again, the company almost solely of other men. In spite of this, he is very at ease with women. In his home life he has been greatly influenced by three generations of women: his mother, his grandmothers and his younger sister. And although it might seem that there has been little time in his life for special attachments, there has been at least one girl to whom, in his schooldays, he was close. ('Her name was Joy,' said my uncle. 'A nice girl. She went to Woodlands.')

Glen loves music, and he's a good dancer. He and Nancy fit well together, even attempting the trickier swing rhythms that force the older, more sedate dancers off the floor. One dance leads to another, and then to the supper table, and the sort of food Glen hasn't seen since he left home, proper country food: sandwiches of all kinds, chicken salad, sausage rolls, egg-and-bacon pies, little iced cakes, scones, slices, jellies, fruit salad and custard, and a constant supply of tea. Food rationing has recently been introduced in Australia (so far restrictions apply to clothing and tea; sugar will be rationed in two days' time, on 29 August), but the culinary skills of the local women are well on display, and the catering is, as expected, excellent.[2]

After supper there is more dancing, very likely with side excursions to partner Nancy's sisters and friends. When at last the band plays 'God Save the King', it is almost three o'clock in the morning, but it seems to both Glen and Nancy that the night has scarcely begun. Already they know, both of them, that they are a couple.

Soon after this, Glen's logbook contains an intriguing

entry. It seems that on 17 September, while flying a CAC Trainer, he made a forced landing at Forbes. He and his passenger, a wireless telegraphy trainee, returned to Parkes on the following day. The reason for the unscheduled landing was not given – it may have been something as simple as running low on fuel. The assessment of the incident was 'nil', and the plane was undamaged. The required Casualty Report was duly signed off by the Commanding Officer at No. 2 Wireless Air Gunners School.

It's very tempting to think that Glen may somehow have managed to see Nancy at this time. He's twenty years old, filled with the spirit of adventure, piloting a plane close to where she lives. And we know that although he's conscientious to a fault, he doesn't *always* follow the rules. (It's less than a year since he was carpeted for ground looping at Western Junction.) But of course this is pure speculation.

The training course at Parkes finished on 31 December 1942, with Glen now promoted from Pilot Officer to Flying Officer. By this time, less than four months after their first meeting, he and Nancy were engaged to be married.

Chapter 17

Engagements and a Wedding

Even in the glow of their happiness, Glen and Nancy must have been aware that wartime romances had the odds stacked against them. There would always be the possibility of separation, with postings at a moment's notice within Australia or overseas. And although nobody wanted to speak of it, being sent into battle meant the constant risk of death or injury, or being taken prisoner-of-war. The stories of what the Japanese did to their prisoners were the stuff of nightmares. By contrast, the Nazis seemed almost civilised. In that way at least, people argued, they were 'like us'. Hated though the Nazis were, the Japanese were hated more. They weren't 'like us', not at all. In caricatures and cartoons they were shown as tiny, ugly, deformed, scrawny, with thick glasses and buck teeth, or with fangs dripping blood. They were 'the murdering Jap', 'the Japanese ape', 'the bloody Nips'.

Britain's disastrous and humiliating loss of Singapore in February 1942, and its subsequent occupation by the Japanese Imperial Army, had dramatically changed the face of the war.[1] It had shown that the previously scorned and ridiculed Japanese forces were in fact strong, disciplined and ruthless, far stronger in South-East Asia than the Allied troops they had so comprehensively outsmarted and defeated. It had been a bitter lesson in reality for the Allies. The appalling savagery of the occupying Japanese against the people of Singapore showed them to be entirely without mercy, fanatical in their aim of creating a new Asia cleansed of Western colonialism.

Nevertheless, the Western media's grotesque cartoonish image of the Japanese soldier remained constant, bolstering the public belief that the 'Nips' could be, and would be, conquered.

As was usual, the graduation of Glen's batch of fellow trainees at Parkes was marked by a celebratory 'passing-out' dinner at the preferred local pub, Tattersall's Hotel. A great deal of light-hearted socialising accompanied all these training courses, with cocktail parties and dances in the officers' mess providing welcome distractions. Undergraduate-style, the wording of the printed graduation program/dinner menu emphasised the drinking of beer and, indeed, passing out. These RAAF graduates, now made battle-ready, could equally be boys leaving school, or graduating from university. Few of them were older than twenty-five.

'They went with songs to the battle,' says the poem, 'they were young,/ Straight of limb, true of eye, steady and aglow.' Young men facing mortality will always attempt to make light of it. There is no other way to bear it, and fear is the burden carried by those who love them.[2]

In December 1942, when Glen and Nancy announced their engagement, my father, now out of the RAAF and back home working for his father on Avon Brae, was preparing to get married. I have a bundle of the letters he wrote to my mother, discussing the plans for their Melbourne wedding and his eager anticipation of the time when at last they could be together. These letters, which I read for the first time only after my mother died, reveal in him a sweetness of character, a sort of innocence, that at first seemed strange to me. Was this gentle, whimsical young man really my father? Of course he was only twenty-six, and he was vulnerable, and hopeful, and in love, but the man who wrote these letters wasn't a bit like the rather distant father I'd known when I was a child. It was only when I was almost grown-up that I had begun to understand and love the complicated, contradictory, essentially endearing person he was beneath that armour of reserve. Now, long after his death, meeting the young man my mother married was a surprise, but a very pleasant one.

Random excerpts from his letters to my mother in the lead-up to their wedding reveal that life on Avon Brae, the life Glen had left behind only eighteen months earlier, but to which he hoped to return, continued as usual.

Darling, a terrifically short note, there's a bush fire just round the corner and I must dash off to it. We fought it for 19 hours last night and this morning, but it still has to be watched very closely. There is a nasty little cross wind blowing and about 150 acres of burning timber.

We have a footrot epidemic here at the moment, methinks it will be with us for quite a while. So far there are about 400 patients, that is the known quantity, there are probably a lot more. It's a pig of a job manicuring sheep all day. I hope the warm weather has a beneficial effect. It usually does.

I'm going to church this afternoon. Mother wants to go, my father doesn't want to go, so Lennie will have to go. I do hope the sermon is fairly short. . . . Mother is having the time of her life. She is organising a Red X fete and has bullied me into collecting stock for it. She insists upon tackling all the old Huns herself tho, she always makes them give something, quite merciless . . .

No more news darling, only 50 more days 1200 hrs or 72000 mins. One Hell of a long time really. It's a great pity that being impatient is one symptom of being in love, there are lots of others too . . .

Must go to bed, have to dip about 900 sheep tomorrow. All my love, dearest heart. Only 48 more days till I see you again.

He worries because he doesn't have a best man for the wedding ceremony, all his friends being in camp or on active service. ('Are attendants necessary?' he writes anxiously to my mother.) In the end his cousin David Miller, a Flight-Lieutenant in the RAAF, takes on the duty of best man and even, so family legend goes, lends the bridegroom a suit to get married in.

As far as I am aware, my father had no other family members at his wedding. Train travel was restricted and expensive, and his parents would have considered it a waste of money to travel to Melbourne just to attend a wedding ceremony, regardless of whose wedding it was. Nor did his sisters attend, for the same reason, nor any of the other people who, if my father had been married in South Australia (or if there were not a war on), would certainly have been there: George and Lulu and their family, for example.

My parents on their wedding day

My parents' wedding day, 5 January 1943, was the day Glen took up his next posting, to the Army Air Squadron at Mascot. Here, because he had shown himself to be a capable and reliable pilot, he was appointed to the Air Communication Flight (ACF). For this posting, which lasted for almost eleven months, he was given the task of flying service personnel, diplomats and other dignitaries all around the country. His logbook lists destinations like Rockhampton, Archerfield, Mackay, Cairns, Cloncurry, Mildura, Coffs Harbour, Cooktown, Amberley and Hughenden; even, twice, Aurukun Mission. Along the way he 'satisfactorily' converted to piloting Airspeed Oxfords, twin-engined aircraft used for training air crews in navigation, wireless-operating, bombing and air gunnery.

During his time at Mascot, Glen was able to widen his experience by flying a range of aircraft – not only the Airspeed Oxfords, but also DH84 Dragons, DH82 Tiger Moths, Avro Ansons, Wirraways, CAC Trainers, DH60 Moth Minors, P40 Kittyhawks, Lockheed Hudsons and Miles Falcons. For this reason he found the posting an especially enjoyable and satisfying one. And although he might be ready for whatever role the RAAF asked of him, he was still in New South Wales, and that was where Nancy was.

Glen's service records show that in August 1943 he was granted combined annual leave and special leave, with an allowance for travelling time. It was almost certainly at this time that he introduced Nancy to his family in Adelaide. As a serviceman, he had priority for travel, with none of the restrictions that applied to civilians.

The meeting of Glen's family and his fiancée was a predictably happy occasion, with immediate rapport on both sides. Nancy was easy to love: warm and approachable, with a ready laugh. The Murries would also have valued the fact that their future daughter-in-law had strong religious faith. To Gwenyth, still a schoolgirl, Nancy was like a glamorous older sister. ('She used to do my hair,' Gwenyth recalls. 'She liked doing people's hair.') On all levels, Nancy's visit to Wandeen was a resounding success.

The Priddles felt a similar affection for Glen. He fitted into their family just as comfortably as Nancy fitted into his. By the time of Glen and Nancy's engagement the Priddles had leased Birangan and were living at East Anglia, a house in Forbes – a move partly dictated by Sydney Priddle's uncertain health.[3] East Anglia soon became Glen's second home. The hospitality of the Priddles was unfailingly generous, and their welcome to the young man loved by their 'baby', their Nancy, was unstinting.

Those glimpses we see of East Anglia in photographs in Nancy's photograph album show that it is a large and comfortable home with a wide return veranda, expansive lawns, roses, banks of hydrangeas, a palm tree, a tennis court.[4] It was the perfect place to relax, free from duties and responsibilities. When he was here with Nancy, the reality of war must have seemed to Glen distant indeed.

While Glen was with the ACF at Mascot, he and Bruce were able to catch up whenever Bruce was on shore leave in Sydney. The brothers stayed at Kinneil, a guesthouse on Elizabeth Bay Road leased by the Australian Comforts Fund as a club for officers of the Australian and Allied forces. Kinneil could accommodate about a hundred officers at a nightly rate (bed and breakfast) of seven shillings and sixpence, with lunch provided at two shillings and sixpence, and dinner at three shillings and sixpence. For entertainment it offered a billiard room, reading and writing rooms, and 'the floor sanded in one room for a dance floor'.[5] There were also fruit machines, which Bruce remembers as the first pokies he'd ever seen. 'They displayed bunches of fruit instead of all the bells and flashing lights of today's machines,' he says. 'It cost sixpence a pop.'

During this time Glen and Nancy managed to see each other as often as they could. The evidence is in the photograph album, in the photos taken by opportunistic street photographers keen to sell their wares to servicemen on leave and their sweethearts. In Nancy they had a prime target, as she eagerly seized the opportunity to record her time with the man she was sure she would spend the rest of her life with.

Here they are, striding confidently down Sydney's streets. Glen is always in uniform, but Nancy, fashionably dressed, is never photographed twice in the same outfit. It's likely that, like many women then, she made at least some of her own clothes. We see her in a checked costume, in a demure long-sleeved dress, in a floral frock with a loose overcoat, in a pale linen suit with a scalloped-edge jacket and a peter pan collar. In this last photo a spray of flowers is pinned to her jacket, and her neat pillbox hat has a veil: perhaps they have just been somewhere special for lunch, or to a wedding. Always she carries gloves and a handbag, the essential armoury of every well-brought-up woman. In none of the photographs are she and Glen holding hands. They are not even touching. Only in one photo are their hands swinging side by side, very close, so close, but still apart. And looking at other photos of the two of them, it's always the same: they are together, but there is a considered distance between them. In those few instances where Glen has his arm around her, or where they are leaning into each other, the camera seems almost to have intruded. Theirs was clearly a deep but very private love, not a love that was on display for everyone to see. To a degree this may have been in deference to the culture of the time, where a woman who showed obvious affection would have been considered 'fast', although that attitude changed dramatically as the war progressed and couples became more openly loving and less cautious. (What was the point of caution when men were away fighting and might never return?) But I suspect that with Glen and Nancy public reticence was also ingrained in their characters. Religion played a large part in their lives – Nancy was Church of England, Glen a committed Baptist – and both were inclined to the observance of niceties, and the sort of behaviour that would be acceptable both to their families and to their Church.

In these street photos, Nancy is usually smiling a small restrained smile, and Glen is either looking straight ahead or away from the camera. There they are, walking down the streets for ever: Nancy bright and assured, Glen more diffident. Opposites, but perfectly in tune with each other. Then I notice something else. In some photographs Nancy is on Glen's left side; in others she is on his right. This, to me, shows that their relationship is still fairly new: they haven't yet established the sort of familiar pattern of walking together that becomes instinctive in a long-established couple. They are still becoming used to each other, still in the exciting time of discovery.

I find myself wishing that in just one of those photographs they were holding hands.

Glen's period of 'General Duties' with the ACF finished on 10 November 1943 (which also happens to be the day my brother was born). His Commanding Officer wrote in his

Nancy and Glen snapped by a street photographer

report that Glen's administrative knowledge was 'weak', but he was otherwise warm in his praise: 'This officer has always been willing and energetic in carrying out his duties, and is very reliable . . . A particularly good, clean type of officer who should always be a credit to the uniform he wears.'

After his eleven-month stint at Mascot, Glen was posted to Forest Hill via Wagga Wagga, an Operational Training Unit (OTU) for twin-engined aircraft. It was closer to Forbes, only 160 miles away, but still more than a three-hour drive. For most pilots, a stint at an OTU was the final training stage before they were posted to a squadron overseas.

Glen's training at No. 5 OTU began on 25 November. He was now flying Bristol Beauforts, which were attack aircraft designed for launching torpedoes and bombing. During the course he would become familiar with the aircraft and its flying characteristics, as well as bombing and air-to-ground gunnery. Bombing practice was stepped up. The possibility of being sent into action was very close now.

Glen put in 53½ hours of flying, including night flying. He signed a statement saying that he had 'been instructed in the methods of operation and limitations of Beaufort type aircraft, and Pratt and Whitney Twin Wasp engines', and was 'fully conversant with Flying Orders as laid down in A.F.O.'s Part 10'.[6]

When the course finished, on 16 January 1944, he was allowed some much-anticipated leave. It would be his last opportunity to spend time with friends and family, and with Nancy, before he left Australia for nine months of service in the Pacific.

For part of his leave Glen stayed at East Anglia, and dozens of black-and-white photographs in Nancy's album record these precious moments. They show the engaged couple together in every conceivable setting: posed on steps, in the garden (backgrounded by flowers, by trees), on the side of a fish pond (with a ceramic frog), on the bank of a river, on a chair (one sitting, the other perched on an arm), in front of a gate. Occasionally they are accompanied by the family dog, an Irish setter. Some of these photos, including many that must have been taken earlier, for none is dated, show them standing with other family members, once or twice with other men in uniform – both RAAF and AIF. Glen himself is so rarely out of uniform that in those few photographs where he is wearing 'mufti', he looks almost unlike himself. The uniform has become an integral part of him, of who he is. For many men the wearing of a uniform was a matter of pride, and this was certainly true in Glen's case.

In several snapshots he and Nancy are sitting together while Nancy cuddles her baby niece, June's daughter Jill, born on 12 November 1943. One photograph shows Glen holding Jill on his knee; in another he is reaching out his hand to her. As they play with the baby, both Glen and Nancy may well be thinking of the family they too will have one day. With Glen's posting overseas now imminent, their plans for marriage have become more pressing. The reality of war, and the danger, can no longer be pushed into the background.

On 5 February 1944 Glen receives the long-awaited news. He is to be deployed to No. 22 Squadron, currently serving in the South West Pacific. His duties are listed, succinctly, as 'Flying'.

From now on Glen will be a bomber pilot on active service. He will be doing what his training has prepared him

Glen, Nancy and baby Jill at East Anglia

for ever since he took his first flight a little over two years ago. Western Junction must now seem to him like primary school, the little Tiger Moth a plaything for children. Doing aerial acrobatics over the soft green Tasmanian countryside is the mildest preparation for what he has to face now.

When the time comes for Glen to catch the train to Sydney, the Priddles farewell him with many expressions of affection and hopes for his safe return. The air is tense with an awareness of possibilities to which nobody will give voice. In a memorably kindly gesture, Sydney Priddle lends his adored youngest daughter the family car (a great privilege) so that she and Glen can drive, just the two of them, to the Forbes railway station.[7]

It's a hot day, and the sun burns down on the station platform. Other people are waiting for the train, but Nancy and Glen scarcely notice them. Nothing seems real but the fact that they are about to part. Each knows how the other feels, but in these last moments together they are deliberately upbeat. They promise to write often. They tell each other how quickly the days will pass: nine months will go in a flash. It won't be long before they are together again.

The train arrives with a burst of steam and a long, harsh squeal of brakes. Passengers climb on board, final goodbyes are said. The guard blows his whistle.

As the train chugs slowly out of the station, Nancy runs back to the car and drives off in the direction of the first level crossing. She will race the train. She and Glen will see each other again – one last time.

She reaches the crossing, stops the car, climbs out. She waits eagerly as the train comes closer and closer. Now it's rattling past, picking up speed, steam flying. And there's Glen, right at the back. He's smiling at her, that beautiful smile; he's waving. Nancy waves back. She waves until the train has snaked away into the distance and she can't see him any more.

Nancy won't cry. Glen wouldn't want her to cry.

She gets back in the car and drives home, alone.

Chapter 18

No. 22 Squadron

No. 22 Squadron, RAAF, was formed on 20 April 1936. It had been involved in the war since the early days, first as a training unit, and then, from June 1942, flying anti-submarine patrols along Australia's east coast. In November 1942 it moved its operations from Richmond, New South Wales, to Port Moresby.[1] By this stage the Japanese had conquered South-East Asia and were fighting for control of the Territory of Papua (at that time governed by an Australian military administration from Port Moresby), Dutch New Guinea and the Solomon Islands.

Initially No. 22 Squadron had operated Ansons and Wirraways, which were then classed by the RAAF as fighter aircraft, but it soon became clear that they were hopelessly outclassed by the Japanese combat planes. From 1942 the squadron began to re-equip with Boston aircraft. It was the only RAAF unit to use the type A28.[2]

The Boston was a twin-engined bomber and attack aircraft used in Europe and the Pacific for low-level strafing and bombing enemy shipping and ground targets. It had a cruise speed of 270 miles per hour and a maximum speed of 300 mph, and it could deliver 1,000 pounds of bombs over a range of 745 miles. Most planes were also armed with four fixed 0.5-inch machine-guns, mounted in the nose.

The Bostons came into service with the RAAF purely by chance. They were never requested, and essentially were seen as stopgap aircraft which would be replaced when more suitable planes became available. The original order for the Bostons was placed by the French Air Force, and after the fall of France in 1940 it was transferred to the RAF. Soon after Japan's entry into the war the order was diverted to the Dutch East Indies, and when Java fell into enemy hands it was diverted yet again, this time to Australia. In March 1942 the first twenty-two aircraft were delivered in crates to Port Melbourne, to be assembled at No. 1 Aircraft Depot, Laverton, and No. 2 Aircraft Depot, Richmond. In the end sixty-nine planes were taken 'on strength' (that is, permanently) by the RAAF between 29 March 1942 and 4 October 1944.

For the RAAF the downside of this unexpected acquisition was that the bombers arrived without the necessary spare parts or any other support material. Because there were few appropriate tools, and the manuals were written in Dutch, the assembly of the planes presented some difficulties for the RAAF ground crews. Maintenance would prove to be an ongoing problem.

For many Australian pilots the Boston Bomber would be the most powerful aircraft they had ever flown. It would also initially be one of the most difficult. Although it was easy to handle, it had a nose wheel, which required different take-off and landing techniques from those most pilots were accustomed to. Designed to carry a crew of three, it usually carried just two – the pilot and his navigator/wireless air gunner or WAG.

In mid-1942 the fortunes of war in the Pacific were fairly

evenly poised. For a while it had seemed that the Allies were fighting a losing battle, but the tide was beginning to turn. Between 4 and 8 May 1942 the US Navy had been victorious against the Japanese in the Battle of the Coral Sea, and soon after that, between 3 and 7 June, in the decisive Battle of the Midway.

In August 1942 the Australians had fought and beaten the Japanese at Milne Bay, on the eastern tip of the Papuan mainland – the first time the enemy had been defeated on land. As a result the Japanese forces were slowly being driven back. They changed their tactics, advancing to the south-west of Papua, capturing the village of Kokoda, and trekking over the Owen Stanley Ranges. From 15 November 1942 the No. 22 Squadron Bostons entered this battle, attacking Japanese positions north-west of Kokoda.

Between 2 and 4 March 1943 No. 22 Squadron played a crucial role in the Battle of the Bismarck Sea, a game-changing air–sea battle in which Allied Air Command virtually wiped out a Japanese convoy of sixteen ships carrying troops and supplies from Rabaul in New Britain to the coastal towns of Lae and Salamaua in New Guinea. The Bostons bombed the enemy convoy, claiming eleven direct hits, and repeatedly attacked the Japanese fighter base at Lae aerodrome, making it much more difficult for the Japanese to provide air cover for their shipping. By the end of the battle the Japanese had lost eight transport ships, five destroyers and at least twenty aircraft. Nearly 3,000 Japanese soldiers and sailors lost their lives.[3]

The operations carried out by the Bostons soon became known as 'Boston Tea Parties'. Some individual aircraft, including Squadron Leader Charles Learmonth's A28-9,

'She's Apples', and Flight-Lieutenant Bill Newton's A28-7, became legendary. Flight-Lieutenant Newton, a brilliant and seemingly fearless pilot, posthumously received the Victoria Cross for continuing to attack the enemy at Salamaua after A28-7 was badly damaged, and then flying it back to base at Port Moresby, 180 miles away, on one engine. He was piloting A28-3 when he was shot down off Salamaua two days later, on 18 March 1943. After ditching in the sea and swimming ashore he was captured by the Japanese and later executed.[4]

In August 1943 the squadron moved from Port Moresby, and until November 1943 it operated from a base at Goodenough Island, east of mainland Papua. The island had been of strategic use to the Japanese forces, but had

Members of No. 22 Squadron. Glen is in the front row, second from left

been successfully taken by the Australians and was declared officially secure by 27 October 1942. By August 1943 it was home to 3,614 RAAF personnel.

When Glen joined No. 22 Squadron in February 1944, it had moved from Goodenough and was based at Kiriwina, the largest of the Trobriand Islands. It was now concentrating its operations in and around the enemy-held areas of New Britain, where it was involved in anti-shipping patrols and attacks around Cape Gloucester. Later its operations were expanded to include photo reconnaissance and ground attack missions on targets throughout New Britain. The airfield at Kiriwina had been constructed by US Army engineers, and with its 6,000 feet of coral-surfaced runway it was regarded as one of the best in the Pacific.

Glen's first sortie was carried out from Kiriwina on 8 March 1944, the day after his twenty-second birthday.[5] In the squadron's Operations Record he is listed as 'Flying Officer Murrie', flying A28-25 in a joint operation with Pilot Officer Sullivan, who was flying A28-23. Their strike mission, which involved several targets in New Britain, was eventful but not entirely successful:

Locate and destroy bridge over tributary of KAPIURA RIVER near UBAI, strafe VISAI VILLAGE. Alternate Target, carry out Visual and Oblique Photo Recce RONDAHL HARBOUR. Primary Target located, 5 x 250 lb. at bridge, all bombs overshot, nil Damage, UBAI VILLAGE strafed, one Jap on pushbike killed, strikes seen on huts. TAROBI strafed, one large European type building left smoking, tracer seen to enter huts. Nil activity WALO ISLAND. At 1,200 feet over MONAGUE

A Boston Bomber coming in to land on Kiriwina airstrip after a bombing and strafing mission *(Photo OG0381, Australian War Memorial)*

[MONTAGU] HARBOUR one explosion which rocked both planes, no burst or smoke seen.

It's easy to imagine Glen's emotions as he set off on his first bombing mission: excitement, almost certainly some trepidation, determination not to fail. Although he had trained for months as a bomber pilot and was completely familiar with the procedures involved, it was the first time he would be putting that knowledge into practice. His WAG on this initial flight was Flying Officer George Rowlands, a stocky, genial former butcher known to everyone as Rowley. The unspecified explosion that rocked their plane would have brought home to Glen with a shock the unpredictability of battle flying, sending his heart into his mouth. Thankfully, no damage was done, but it must have been a great relief to him when he landed A28-25 safely on Kiriwina airstrip.

His next mission, on 25 March, was to bomb and strafe Bialla Plantation, a 'suspected camp of Japs':

. . . bombed and strafed by 3 Bostons, bombing excellent, 116 Fragmentation Bombs dropped covering Plantation area. Track from KIAVA to GALUPEI strafed . . . 9,300 Japanese, 3,000 Native leaflets dropped BIALLA area. Photos taken of BIALLA.

Again, Glen's WAG was Rowley. The bond between a pilot and his 'second' was a vital one, and throughout the months ahead Rowley regularly crewed for Glen. They became a team of the kind so often forged in extreme circumstances: reliable, mutually loyal, and, in the way of close friends and workmates, familiar with each other's quirks and foibles.

In March 1944 the squadron was assigned to No. 77 Wing, together with No. 30 and No. 31 Squadrons. No. 77 Wing, the attack component of the RAAF's No. 10 Operational Group, had been established on 13 November 1943 with headquarters at Nadzab in the Markham Valley, near Lae. The group was effectively a mobile strike force designed to support Allied ground and naval units while they advanced against the Japanese in the south-west Pacific area.

In August 1944 No. 22 Squadron relocated yet again, this time to Noemfoor (now Numfor) Island in Dutch New Guinea, just north and to the western end of the New Guinea mainland.[6]

Noemfoor is a small oval-shaped island covering an area of approximately 130 square miles and almost entirely surrounded by a ring of coral reefs. It consists of a series of limestone and coral terraces, with narrow beaches interspersed with mangrove swamps. Inland, its rugged terrain is covered with dense rainforest. In 1944 it had an indigenous population of about 5,000 living in small coastal villages and eking out a subsistence lifestyle. There were also just over a thousand Formosans and Indonesians, survivors of more than 4,000 brought there by the Japanese and used as slave labour to construct roads and airfields, almost entirely by hand. Three airfields were built on the island, turning it into a major air base. It was used mainly as a staging point for Japanese troops being sent to reinforce a detachment of about 11,000 on Biak, a much bigger and strategically more important island to the east of Noemfoor.

American and Australian air forces had started bombing Noemfoor on April 1944, and from 2 July Allied units began to land around Kamiri airstrip on the north-west of the island. The Japanese launched a counter-attack, but were unsuccessful, and the Allies declared Noemfoor secure on 7 July. Later that month No. 77 Wing relocated its headquarters to the island.

The No. 22 Squadron Bostons arrived on Kamiri airstrip on 10 and 11 August.

Glen's first operation out of Noemfoor, on 16 August 1944, was to pilot one of four Bostons attacking possible enemy headquarters at Saonek Island.

Bombing excellent, says the report. *16 bombs dropped seen to burst in centre of building area. Two direct hits on iron-roofed buildings . . . Thick black smoke to 1500' & increasing in density visible for 30 miles . . .*

Boston aircraft of No. 22 Squadron on Kamiri airstrip, August 1944
(Photo OG1517, Australian War Memorial)

For the first time Glen is listed in the Operations Records as 'Flight-Lieutenant Murrie'. He had been promoted with effect from 30 April.

At this time Dutch New Guinea and the scattering of islands further to the west were all enemy occupied. Together with No. 30 Squadron, which flew Bristol Beaufighters, No. 22 Squadron was given the task of bombing and strafing enemy shipping in the area, as well as ground targets like airfields, troop concentrations and munitions dumps. Because the Bostons had a longer range, they were used particularly against airfields on Ceram and in the Kai (now Kei) Islands of the Dutch East Indies, and for barge sweeps. The Japanese used long barges to transport troops and supplies, and these were obvious targets.

The Boston attacks were frequently successful, and the bomber crews took great pride in their achievements, recording their hits with multiple images of bombs painted on the sides of their aircraft. Each hit took them a step closer to winning the war, and that was an outcome that couldn't happen soon enough. But their sorties were always dangerous.

Air crew and ground staff on the Noemfoor base made up a sizeable community, essentially a working town. Accommodation was fairly basic. All fixed buildings were made of wood, but the men lived under canvas, sleeping in bunk beds in large tents with raised timber floors. A few personal possessions helped to create a feeling of home, and vegetable gardens were established in the surrounding areas. There were communal living areas, a kitchen, a medical tent. Meals were eaten in a large mess tent. A padre, or chaplain, conducted regular church services. He also had the mournful duty of conducting burial services for servicemen killed in action – those whose bodies could be found – and writing letters of condolence to their families.

Efficiency, co-operation and that indefinable quality known in Australia as mateship were key to the squadron's success. At the time Glen joined it, morale was high, and a sense of pride in the unit and its achievements was felt by everyone involved, from cooks and mechanics to the pilots and their crews. The men knew the importance of what they were doing, and they made a concerted effort to keep dark thoughts at bay. Still, they could not be unaware of the risks involved. Added to this, they were all far from home, and compelled to live in unfamiliar and often uncomfortable conditions.

Nothing could be done about the danger or the isolation

or the extremes of tropical weather, and not much could be done about the mosquitoes, but life was made as pleasant as possible. Fresh food supplies and eagerly awaited mail-bags were brought in by the Lockheed Lodestar aircraft of No. 37 Squadron, the RAAF transport unit. And there were many diversions. Occasionally a cricket match was played on Kamiri airstrip, although generally speaking the relentless humidity made sports a less attractive option. The men kept their spirits up with impromptu concerts, regular open-air picture nights, card games, two-up, and writing letters.[7]

Glen and one of the squadron's Bostons. Like many in the RAAF he has grown a moustache. In a letter to Lulu dated 12 October 1944 Nancy mentions a photo she has received – perhaps this one: 'It was a lovely clear photo but not terribly like Glen with the "mo" – how we have laughed about his "mo's" . . .'

This was Glen's life now, and it was a world away from Nancy's, both physically and mentally. When he was on a mission he was completely focused, using all his skill to achieve his targets; when he was off duty he gave just as much in a personal way, being involved in activities, being part of the team. He was seen as a future leader, even on occasion acting as the squadron's Commanding Officer. One of his regular duties was to help the chaplain by reading from the Scriptures at Sunday services and playing the piano for hymn singing. (I imagine that his talent as a pianist was frequently sought on livelier occasions, too.) This sort of co-operative spirit was something that came naturally to him, part of both his upbringing and his faith. He was also by now very used to the communal life of a military base, with its mixture of cheerful camaraderie and enforced privation. Friendships forged in the difficult circumstances of wartime, when people are without the immediate support of family and loved ones, have a unique depth, and Glen was a good friend to many. Although he was by nature rather reserved, he was greatly liked. He had the sort of quiet strength that others looked up to.

Nancy wrote to Glen every day. She wrote about her home, her family, local gossip, wedding plans, their future together. In the adrenaline-fuelled, wholly male world he now inhabited, her letters were his lifeline to home and peaceful domestic reality. Both were looking forward to their wedding. It was planned to take place at the end of November, immediately after Glen's return from his nine months of active service.

Nancy had already selected her wedding dress, a slender, silky, lacy thing with puffed sleeves and a peter pan collar. Her veil was edged with lace and embroidery. Many clothing coupons had been saved up to make possible the purchase of these bits of finery. The church had been booked, and details of the reception had been finalised. It would be a typical country wedding, with guests arriving at Forbes from considerable distances, and hospitality in friendly abundance. All that was missing was the bridegroom, and he would be home now within weeks.

Nancy's parents had been planning in secret for the future of the newlyweds. They intended to set them up on a farm. It would be the perfect start for them – a place where Nancy could be close to her family, and where Glen could put to use all he had learned at Avon Brae. It seemed a lifetime ago, but in fact it was only three years since he had described his occupation as 'sheep farmer'. Glen loved flying: it fulfilled something deep inside him, and he gave it every bit of his dedication and concentration. All the same, he must often have hungered for the time when he could trade the excitement and danger of being a bomber pilot for the quieter challenges of living on the land.

With their own youthful energy and plenty of willing help from the family, he and Nancy could build a life for themselves and the children they expected to have. Nancy wanted children. Her adoration of Jill, June's baby daughter, confirmed her longing to have babies of her own.

Although she was only twenty-one, Nancy's course in life was set. Like many young women of her generation, she wanted nothing more than to share her life with the man she loved. It was a dream that was now tantalisingly close to reality.

Chapter 19

On Active Service

The words 'bomber pilot' conjure up all sorts of romantic notions, but an examination of the No. 22 Squadron records reveals the less glamorous truth that although it's a hazardous job, it is in effect just a job. After a while, the bombing missions become almost routine. There are things that need to be done, and people trained to do them; and they must be accomplished as efficiently and safely as possible. Wastage of resources – whether planes or people or bombs – is to be avoided wherever possible.

The squadron's official record of operations is divided into sections: Date, Base, Aircraft Type (always 'Boston'), Aircraft Number, Rank, Pilot, Time Up/Time Down, Mission, Description of Operation. It reveals that bombing raids were conducted on buildings, on air strips, on bridges, on transport barges, on munitions dumps, on troop concentrations, on villages that might be harbouring the enemy. There were reconnaissance flights, flights attempting to locate enemy destroyers, flights to protect Allied shipping, flights to drop leaflets (psychological warfare). At the end of each Description of Operation there is a brief breakdown of ordnance: the bombs used, those lost, those returned to base.[1]

Each mission started out in more or less the same way

'Pilots standing beside an aircraft . . . of No. 22 (Boston Bomber) Squadron RAAF checking over the course on the maps before setting out on a strike over enemy territory.' From left, the pilots are Flight-Lieutenant Robert, Glen, Flying Officer Ford, Flight-Lieutenants Williamson and Daly, and Flying Officer Warren *(Photo OG1529, Australian War Memorial)*

with issuing orders, selecting planes and crews, checking the course on maps. Did the tension of waiting, and the overwhelming weight of expectation, ever recall to Glen the moments before he rowed for his school? Now, instead of the gentle breeze over the Torrens Lake, there was the glare of tropical sun on the runway, the suffocating humidity, the clunk as bombs were loaded into the aircraft bomb racks. Then the suiting up in flying gear and life-jackets, climbing aboard, and the deafening roar as the Boston engines burst into life, one after another, in a noisy cacophony. Once aloft, the tension drained away, but then there were other things to be borne: the discomfort of being in a noisy, hot, stuffy cockpit for hours on end, knowing that anti-aircraft fire could pepper the plane at any moment, being constantly alert to any small changes in the familiar sound of the engines. The Bostons, with their chequered history, were prone to sudden failure. The squadron's Operations Records show that on several occasions missions were aborted because of a problem with the aircraft.

There were other problems. Apart from the constant risk of anti-aircraft attack, the records reveal that missions were frequently compromised by fuel shortages, poor weather conditions, 'meagre light', bombs overshot or undershot.

The dozens of missions in which Glen took part were usually carried out by groups of planes, and covered the full range of bombing and strafing actions. A small selection from the records describes some typical operations:

20 August 1944: Five Bostons strike targets of opportunity SAGAN & OTAWARI AREA. 100% coverage. One canoe heading west in direction of BABO carrying five Japs strafed and sunk approx. 5 miles off CAPE KABARISI. Direct hit on BABO debris to 200' . . . Did not complete sweep due to W/T [wireless telegraphy] trouble . . . 10 x 100 lb, 8 x 500 lb, 5,400 .5 on targets.

23 August 1944: Eight Bostons bomb OTAWIRI strip. Excellent 32 bombs dropped completely covered strip from end to end. 12 x 500 lbs 12 x 100. 8 x 250 on target.

27 August 1944. Four Bostons sweep South Coast of CERAM. Coast swept from BAY of WAROE to CAPE KILBON. Two bombs on heavily camouflaged barge off shore in BAY of WAROE. One direct hit. Four bombs on five boats. Five strafing runs hits seen. Two Japs at mouth of MASIWANG RIVER strafed. Seven strafing runs on two 60' schooners off CAPE KILBON hits seen on both. Two barges heavily camouflaged mouth of KAMARIN RIVER strafed hits slight smoke from one . . . Two Bostons did not sweep due to engine trouble. 8,000 leaflets dropped in CAPE KILBON area. 500 dropped GOELIGPILE. 4 x 500lb 4 x 100 – 6,600 x .5 on targets. 2 x 500 2 x 100 jettisoned. 2 x 100 returned to base.

04 September 1944: Six Bostons attack WAHAI VILLAGE. Mission incomplete due to adverse weather . . .

The names of the pilots recur in apparently random rotation: Flight-Lieutenant Daly, Flight-Lieutenant Robert, Flying Officer Atkins, Flying Officer Davidson, Pilot Officer Collett, Flight-Lieutenant Murrie, Flying Officer Raynor, Pilot Officer Sullivan, Flying Officer Rennison. More and more of them, differently ranked, frequently promoted, all of them young, some with little experience of 'flying battle'. Occasionally Squadron Leader Colin Woodman appears in the mix, and Wing Commander Hickey, leading from the front.

Inevitably there were occasional incidents when, as a result of inattention, inexperience, or sheer bad luck, individual aircraft suffered damage because of mechanical fault or pilot error. On 17 August, according to the squadron's records, A28-56 was forced to crash-land at base because of hydraulic trouble; four days later 'A28-64 hit trees with Port Motor, returned safely to base'. On 28 August A28-55, piloted by Flying Officer Frank Ford, struck a tree on take-off and returned to base 'unserviceable'. Luckily, in none of these incidents was anybody injured.

Although they were constantly in harm's way, the Boston crews had been leading a charmed life for several months, with no casualties. Suddenly, that was to change.

The squadron's month of horrors began on 5 September. On that day seven Bostons were engaged in one of many repeat missions to bomb Boela airstrip, on the north-eastern tip of Ceram, and the Japanese-occupied oil refinery there. The Bostons were hit by 'slight to medium' anti-aircraft fire: A28-63 was hit in the port nacelle and in the fuselage from turret to tail. When it landed back at base, its brakes failed and it hit a moving truck. The aircraft was a complete wreck, but miraculously the crew was unhurt.

They were fortunate that time, but before long the squadron was dogged by disaster.

On 14 September five men were lost on a non-operational flight. Service records show that A28-61 took off from Kamiri airstrip at 1553 hours. A test flight had been authorised to check adjustments made to its electrical system, following 'complete electrical failure' on its previous flight. The plane was piloted by twenty-three-year-old Flying Officer James Davidson. Also on board were navigator Warrant Officer Wallis Glew and three passengers. These three, a fitter and two flight mechanics, were Leading Aircraftmen Charles Bone, William Costigan and Frank Street.

The aircraft took off without incident, completed a right-hand turn, and flew off in a northerly direction. Half an hour later, to the increasing consternation of those back at the base, it had not returned. Their worst fears were confirmed when a crew member aboard HMAS *Gympie*, which was patrolling in the area, reported that he had seen an unidentified aircraft crash into the sea four or five miles north-east of Noemfoor.

As the plane had gone down so near to base, a thorough search by air and sea was mounted straight away. Even the US 34th Fighter Sector was called into action. Receiving notification of the crash from the navy, the sector Controller, Lieutenant Allan Wise, Jr, 'despatched two Peters from 78 Squadron, one Sugar from 22 Squadron and one Littleboy to search the area, but they returned at last light and reported nil sightings'. A great deal of flotsam was found in the area, but nothing resembling aircraft wreckage, and crucially there was no oil slick to indicate the exact position of the crash. The search continued until darkness fell. There was no sign of survivors.

The next day, deciding that it was crucial for the few witnesses to be interviewed as soon as possible, the squadron's Commanding Officer, Squadron Leader Colin Woodman, assigned an investigating officer to the case. The officer he selected for this task was Glen, who, as it happened, had also authorised the test flight.

During the course of the investigation Glen interviewed eight people, four of them ground staff – electricians and fitters.[2] Two of these men testified that they had been in the dispersal bay at the time A28-61 taxied out, and had seen nothing to cause them any concern. All four confirmed that the plane had been passed as fit for flying. Glen himself was not required to testify.

The clearest account of the incident was that given by nineteen-year-old Able Bodied Seaman Ronald Shiers, the sailor on board HMAS *Gympie*. His sworn statement was witnessed by Glen and countersigned by Flying Officer John Warren.

At 1557 hours on the 14th September I was on duty on the bridge head and spotted an aircraft about 8 miles distant on a bearing 045 degs from Noemfoor. The aircraft was too far away to positively identify but appeared to have two black markings each side of the fuselage and was at low altitude at the time of sighting. The aircraft was rolling at the time and losing height rapidly, the flash of the sun on the wings attracting my attention. The aircraft hit the water in a nose down attitude and a great spout of water shot up and it disappeared almost immediately.

The 'black marks' may have been smoke. According to a report received by the control tower and later noted in his deposition by Commanding Officer Woodman, the aircraft was 'apparently on fire'.

Following the interviews, Glen's investigation revealed that nothing had been amiss, and no blame attached to any personnel. The documentation of the test flight was checked by Commanding Officer Woodman, and the test was found to have been correctly authorised. Flying Officer Davidson had only a relatively brief 98 hours and 55 minutes' solo flying experience, but it was enough to qualify him to pilot a Boston. The squadron's Medical Officer testified that the young pilot was perfectly fit, and had not been suffering from fatigue. Similarly, A28-61 was found to have been 'serviceable in every respect for flying'. None of the relevant logbooks revealed any defects that could have caused the accident.

The reason for the aircraft crashing just four minutes after takeoff, possibly on fire, was never discovered. Nevertheless, in the absence of enemy attack or bad weather, it is difficult not to draw the conclusion that the crash was caused either by pilot error or aircraft failure.

On 18 September A28-55 was back in the air, repaired and cleared for service after its ignominious collision with a tree on 28 August. Glen was the pilot on this first post-repair flight, a dawn attack mission with ten other aircraft searching for enemy destroyers. (*Search carried out as ordered. Nil enemy sightings.*)

On 20 September five Bostons flew off to bomb that now familiar target, Boela airstrip. Glen was again flying A28-55. The Bostons left at 0740 hours, and came back at 1240. Or rather, four of them came back, because the pilot of A28-53, twenty-year-old Flying Officer Henry Atkins, and his WAG, Pilot Officer Ronald Gehrmann, failed to return to base. Two days later the burnt-out remains of A28-53 were discovered in jungle on Gorong Island, where it had apparently exploded on impact.

These losses, so close together, must have had a profound effect on the morale of No. 22 Squadron. Earlier in the war, aircraft had gone missing or been shot down, like Bill Newton's A28-3, but for seven-and-a-half months the squadron had not lost a plane, or a man. There had been accidents and near-misses, but never the chilling *Aircraft failed to return*. Until the loss of A28-61 on 14 September the squadron's last flying fatality had been at Kiriwina on 30 January, when Wing Commander James Emerton and his WAG, Pilot Officer Terence Gawne, crashed while carrying out a barge sweep. Witnesses saw their port motor burst into flames, and photographs were taken of the burning aircraft. 'Ack ack' (anti-aircraft) fire was suspected but not confirmed: possibly Emerton was shot. But that had happened in what passes during wartime for 'long ago', just before Glen had joined the squadron. Now the crashes of A28-61 and A28-53, neither of them fully explained, were blunt reminders that in air warfare there is often only the smallest of margins – call it fate, chance, or blind luck – between survival and disaster.

Flying bombers, and especially flying Bostons, often involves low-level flying. Glen may have found low flying in a Tiger Moth 'extra good', but in a bomber it is extremely hazardous. Should anything go badly wrong, there is little a pilot can do to save either himself and his crew, or his aircraft. If the only option is to bail out, there may not be sufficient space or time to allow a parachute to open. And if the plane is flying over sea or dense forest or rugged mountains, a safe landing is virtually impossible. All the squadron's pilots were aware of this; few, probably, would have dwelt on it.

On 23 September four Bostons were scheduled to take part in barge sweeps around the Kai Islands. Glen, piloting A28-55, was to be the leader of the formation. The other pilots rostered were his friend Flight-Lieutenant David Daly, and Flying Officers Dargan McKenzie and John Warren. Glen would be accompanied by his usual trusted WAG, Rowley.

Glen and Rowley

The Kai Islands were 350 miles away from base, so it was a gruelling five-hour operation, with the Bostons due to leave Noemfoor at 0800 hours and return at 1300 hours.

The morning of 23 September was sultry and overcast, with humidity pushing 90 and air temperature already at 75 degrees. After breakfast the four crews discussed details of the day's operation. The briefing was soon over: this was considered a fairly routine strike mission.

Out on the airstrip there was scarcely any wind. Rain threatened, with clouds already beginning to mass on the horizon. Against the pale grey sky, the tropical rainforest was vividly green.

It was an ordinary, normal morning: as usual, everything was on schedule. There were final inspections of the aircraft. Last-minute chiacking from the ground crews. Cheerful farewells. Life-jackets on, hatches closed. The familiar petrol smell of the cockpit. Engines coming to life, sputtering at first, and then roaring.

The four aircraft took off in formation, Glen leading the way in A28-55. He settled into the flight. Endless sea, endless sky, the reassuring steady growl of the Boston's powerful Wright Cyclone engines. The sporadic crackling of the radio as Rowley made contact from the gunner's enclosure at the rear of the aircraft, occasionally relieving the tedium with a joke.

When Glen had completed the first section of his sweep and was turning out to sea, flying low, the unthinkable happened. At a distance of about a hundred yards Flying Officer McKenzie, piloting the accompanying Boston, A28-57, watched in horror as smoke began to issue from Glen's cockpit. Soon A28-55 was engulfed in flames and rapidly losing height. The aircraft crashed into the sea. In seconds the water had closed over it.

Flying Officer McKenzie circled the area repeatedly, but could see no trace of either the plane or its crew. A fuel tank and a half-inflated dinghy were spotted immediately after the crash, but that was all. Running low on fuel now, A28-57 was forced to head back to base.

Their fellow squadron members would have received the terrible news about Glen and Rowley with shock, sadness and disbelief, but also, probably, with a degree of fatalism. If your number was up, that was it; and all the men knew it. Some may well have wondered, without saying it, who would be next.

We still don't know for certain why A28-55 burst into flames. It could have been enemy fire – on all the evidence this is the most probable reason – or it could have been a failure of the aircraft itself. As the only witness interviewed, Flying Officer McKenzie could give no definitive explanation.

It is worth noting, however, that sudden explosions of flame, for reasons not entirely clear, had recently caused the loss of two other Bostons – A28-53 and A28-61. And on 25 September the squadron would lose yet another plane, yet another crew, when Flying Officers John Warren and Kenneth Clark, in A28-50, crashed into the sea near the Aroe (now Aru) Islands. The circumstances of the crash were similar to those apparently experienced by Glen and Rowley. (*No sign of survivors. Crews consider possibly Pilot hit by A/A.*)

Unlike the first Bostons flown by No. 22 Squadron, all these planes were A-20G models, American built. In mid-1944 the squadron, by now reduced to only ten operational aircraft, had been re-equipped and given an entirely new look with Bostons on loan from the US Air Force. The A-20Gs flew in the standard US colour scheme of olive drab with medium green over neutral grey. Following the arrival of these aircraft on Noemfoor there was a dramatic increase in the number of operations carried out.[3] This alone, statistically, made casualties more likely.

In September A28-50, A28-53 and A28-55 were still relatively new planes, all of them having been delivered to Noemfoor in June 1944. A28-61 was taken on a month later. At the time they crashed, A28-50 had flown eighteen missions, A28-53 fifteen, A28-55 eleven, and A28-61 only four.[4] It's not impossible that there was an undiscovered mechanical or electrical fault common to some or all of these aircraft. We know that in the case of A28-61, at least, enemy action was out of the question.

It is also worth noting that A28-55 had been rendered 'unserviceable' after its accident less than four weeks earlier. Was it correctly repaired and fit for service? There is no evidence that it wasn't, and now, seven decades later, nothing can be either proved or disproved. But a tiny doubt remains.

In the Flying Casualty report on the loss of A28-55, Glen was still not officially listed as dead. 'It is considered that both members of the crew would have been killed as a result of the crash,' wrote Commanding Officer Woodman in his Confirmatory Memorandum dated 29 September, 'but owing to lack of confirmation of this, both members of the crew are posted "missing believed killed".' The memorandum finishes with a brief account of Glen's career as a pilot. He was listed as having 1100.55 flying hours. His flying assessment at SFTS was above average. His last flying assessment was above average. The unit's assessment was above average.[5]

It is a dry, impersonal summary. But in wartime death is common, and it must be kept within formal parameters. In a war, as on a farm, there is little room for sentiment.

In less than two weeks No. 22 Squadron had seen the loss of four planes and eleven men.

I have in front of me Glen's logbook, the pages filled in with his careful handwriting. I imagine him, each evening, writing up the day's duties with his fountain pen (no biros then). The entries are scrupulously up to date, recorded in small, precise capital letters, as neat as typescript. And here is the last entry.

Year: 1944. Month: SEPT. Date: 22. Aircraft type: A20 G BOSTON. No. A28-54. Pilot, or 1st Pilot: F/L MURRIE. 2nd Pilot, Pupil or Passenger: F/O ROWLANDS. Duty (Including Results and Remarks): TEST.

On the facing page are listed the technical details of the test flight, followed by the stamp and signature of Commanding Officer Colin Woodman.

And after that, nothing.

Chapter 20

Missing

The telegram saying that Glen was missing was delivered to Wandeen by a boy on a bicycle. Like Glen himself only a few years earlier, he was probably making a little pocket money during the school holidays. The front door was opened by Gwenyth, who was then fifteen years old. When she received the telegram and saw that it was marked 'urgent', she feared the worst.

It is difficult for us now, so used to instant communication, to comprehend the aching slowness of written correspondence. Even 'wires' were prone to delays, and were far from immediate. The telegram from RAAF headquarters in Melbourne, dated 27 September, finally arrived at Glen's home in Hazelwood Park four days after his death. Four days in which those who loved him went calmly about their daily lives, oblivious to what had happened.

Gwenyth, who is now in her eighties, still remembers with great clarity the moment she answered the knock on the door and received the telegram. Typically she remarked how sorry she felt for the delivery boy. Little more than a child, he had the terrible task of taking these grim messages to families with sons and daughters in the services, seeing the instant fear on their faces, and witnessing their heartbroken reactions.

George and Lulu had planned to go to the movies, and they were in the car, about to drive out, when Gwenyth raced up to the garage to forestall them. The sight of the yellow paper in her hand must have made their hearts leap with terror, and then sink.

DEEPLY REGRET TO INFORM YOU THAT YOUR SON 416600 FLIGHT LIEUTENANT GLEN INGLIS MURRIE IS MISSING BUT BELIEVED TO HAVE LOST HIS LIFE ON 23RD SEPTEMBER 1944 AS RESULT OF AIR OPERATIONS STOP . . . FAILED TO RETURN TO BASE STOP THE MINISTER FOR AIR JOINS WITH AIR BOARD IN EXPRESSING SINCERE SYMPATHY IN YOUR ANXIETY STOP WHEN ANY FURTHER INFORMATION IS RECEIVED IT WILL BE CONVEYED TO YOU IMMEDIATELY.[1]

All three of them would have pored over the words, again and again. 'Believed to have lost his life'. '*Believed*', not '*known*'. And the dread word 'killed' had not been used. There was still hope, then. Not much, but a little.

A memorandum on Letters of Condolence from the No. 5 Base Personnel Staff Office clarifies the reason for this lack of directness: 'It is essential that any expression of sympathy must correspond to the nature of the casualty in deference to the feelings of the next of kin, and in order not to create despair in their minds, statements inferring that the members have been killed are not to be mentioned. It is advised that R.A.A.F. Headquarters is the only body empowered to presume the members dead, and do so through official channels.'[2]

In spite of its avowed intention not to create despair, this policy often had the opposite effect. Many, if not most, would have preferred to know the truth. To allow for hope when in fact there is none is cruel indeed.

That night George had the terrible task of telephoning Nancy with the news.

For Nancy it was virtually a mortal blow. In her letter to Lulu, written on Thursday 28 September, her efforts to be rational and to have faith struggle against the grief and pain that would soon all but bury her. Above all there is a feeling of bewilderment, of disbelief. The letter leaps from one point to another, picks up a thought, discards it, leaps to another. Nancy isn't thinking clearly. She *can't* think clearly. But like the Murries, she is a committed Christian, and her belief provides a small degree of comfort. She must have prayed hard for strength and guidance. Drawing on this, and realising that hers is not the only loss – that Lulu and George have lost their son – she takes on the role of comforter.

My Dearest Mrs Murrie, wrote twenty-one-year-old Nancy,

There's really nothing much I can say today but to send you my love.

You were very brave on the phone this morning & I feel better since hearing your voice.

Poor little Gwenyth, what a shock for her.

I don't want you to think I haven't any faith, but from the wording of the wire I do feel we would be unkind to each other to have false hopes.

The first thing I said to Mummy was, he's too good for this world. However I feel lucky to have had him for so long.

He was happy until the last & I know that God would

not have let him be any other way at the end. I know in my head that whatever did happen, was sudden & painless.

I dozed off this morning & dreamt Glen came to us today & said "Don't cry, don't cry, little Jill will soon be here & I might be back" & he was gone.

I am worried about Dear old Daddy, his heart isn't the best & I don't know how he will take it but we are only going to say he is missing. There is all the difference in the world between "missing" & "missing & believed killed" for they usually only report the first unless they know something.

So after all it was our Boston that was lost, I never thought Glen would go – he was such a good & careful pilot, but it must have been anti aircraft fire. I sent wires to Rennison, Daly & Raynor & asked them to write & send photographs if they could.

Mummy wants you to come over but I know you all couldn't come & you wouldn't separate now so I think I shall go over. I just don't know what to do but I feel I want to see you all.

Well My Dear I must close, I've never thought this would happen & I still can't realize it.

Vic is on the phone & June is ill today & can't come so I won't have little Jill as Glen told me, after all, but Juney can't come if she's sick, poor little thing will want to be with us now, she too just idolized Glen.

Goodbye for the present & I'll write tomorrow.

My love to each and every one of you and I hope Bruce is home to help you over your sorrow.

Fondest love & all my sympathy,

Nancy

At that time telephones were used mainly for emergencies. Trunk calls, which had to be booked in advance through the telephone exchange, were fairly rare on a private level, and often signified bad news. When Nancy took the call from Adelaide, she must have suspected at once that something terrible had happened.

Slowly the information began to sink in. Nancy's next letter to Lulu, written only hours after the previous one ('Thursday night, 28/9/44'), shows that numbing shock is starting to give way to comprehension. In her feeling of helplessness and loss Nancy turns to Glen's family, thinking that to be near them is next best to being with him. The letter is blotted here and there with tears.

Dearest Mrs Murrie,

All I feel like is writing to you but when I start I just don't know what to say.

It has been a dreadful day for us all & my one regret is that we could not be together as Glen would have liked that but I am going to see you soon.

We are having a memorial service for Glen on Saturday morning in the Church of England, Padre came this morning & spoke to me beautifully & I must try to do the things he said, I do feel Glen very near to me & as Padre says I must not think this is the end but look forward to our wedding in heaven.

. . . I wish Daddy and Juney were home, in fact I'm longing to see them more than they realize but June is very sick & cannot come home until Monday week & we are trying to get Daddy home as soon as possible without alarming him.

I'll have to write more about this when we both feel more settled, but I want to go over in about two weeks time, if you are thinking of all going away for a holiday, why not come here but I must see you.

Am longing to get your lettergram tomorrow & then your letters – tomorrow – the 29th – just two months from our wedding day, it is certainly hard to take but Glen would want us to be brave & I'm doing my best for his sake.

I am addressing this to you but mean it for you all & am longing to see each one of you, I thought I was the luckiest girl in the world having you for inlaws, but unless by some unlikely miracle it seems we are only to be friends, although you are more than that to me.

Well my Dear I must say goodnight now – the thought of another endless night nearly breaks my heart but it will be a wound for time to heal.

My fond and loving thoughts are with you

Your everloving Nancy

The letters come tumbling out. On the next day, 29 September, she writes to Gwenyth the sort of affectionate, confiding letter a big sister would write to a younger one. With almost unbearable poignancy, she writes, '. . . my Glen came to me again in my sleep & told me not to write to him again as he wouldn't have time to answer my letters, I know he has gone but his spirit is with me & I'm trying to be brave as I know it is his wish'.

She speaks of the wedding that now will never take place:

I too have had beautiful flowers sent to me, I have Glen's big smiling photograph surrounded with lilac . . . Everyone in Forbes loved Glen & were looking forward to our wedding – two months from today – one of our friends told Mummy this morning she was getting ready for a pre-wedding party for me when she heard the news. I am going to bring my frock and veil over to show you as I feel Glen would like me to do that.

Glen said he was going to write & tell you we bought our wedding ring in Adelaide but were going to keep it a secret until we had decided definitely, I don't know whether he did tell you, but I am going to wear it on my right hand, it is a beautiful little ring & has brought me much happiness.

We must feel proud of Glen & try & be brave & make ourselves worthy of the sacrifice he has made.

I think your Mother has the greatest burden to carry, she had reared Glen to the perfection he was & it was that which I loved for the last two years.

I knew this world was not good enough for Glen but prayed that he might be spared to play his part in making it a better world, but he has played his part & no one could have given more than he has – except your Father & Mother who gave their son.

Already she is thinking of joining one of the forces to help with the war effort, both to keep herself occupied and as a tribute to Glen:

Mummy will take me over to see you & stay a few days with your Mother & I shall stay a while longer, after

Nancy's wedding dress

which I don't know what I'll do, but know I cannot live in Forbes & go back to the office. I want to be doing something to make my life more useful. I can't join the Army or Air Force on account of their rookie courses & every time I have tried to join the W.R.A.N.S. in Sydney they have not been recruiting, but I shall see them in Adelaide & they may take me there & send me back to Sydney. I wish you were older so that we could do something together as I feel any one of you are the next best thing.

She casts wildly around in her mind for ways in which she might, as people now say, 'move on', while at the same time all she wants to do is to look back. Her days of happiness with Glen are gone, and her future with him is over before it has begun. 'I still can't realize he may never come back,' she writes to Lulu on 2 October, '& although it fills my thoughts all the time, there are often little incidents which happen & I think "I must tell Glen when I write" & it comes as a shock again.'

Lulu's letters to Nancy have not survived – or if they have survived, I haven't seen them – but it is easy to imagine that she wrote to the girl who would have been her daughter-in-law with enormous empathy and kindness, occasionally offering wise practical advice. The letters from Bertha Priddle, Nancy's mother, are openly emotional. 'We are just heartbroken over the loss of our darling,' she writes to Lulu on the Saturday after the news was received. 'As my Nancy said "mother he was too good to live" and I have often thought he just was too good for this world, and how happy I used to be, that he was the one appointed to care for my girlie through life. – Poor little Pet has been so brave. But I had often said to Glen, I do wish Nan did not love so much.'

Bye & Bye, she continues, *we will go down [to Adelaide] for a little while – that is all that Nan wishes for – her heart is just where he was – his home that he loved so much*

Nance had told you a little of what we have talked

over here as to their future – that was to be – we were just waiting till you and Mr Murrie & our dear Glen were all here with us to discuss it all

Well such lots & lots we have had to do of late we just were so full of jobs – and now we just feel we have nothing to do, all our plans were for "Just Before" or Just After – or at the Wedding . . .

You would be very proud of our Nan. She has been so Brave. They have always said I spoilt my baby – that they were always teasing dear Glen & saying they were sorry for him. My! She has been a little Brick . . . I fear for further trouble with her, as she is trying to be just as she promised Glen if the worst ever came. Each night she has dreamt of him . . . just that he comes to her & speaks some advice . . .

Every night my dear just sat and wrote pages & pages to him. All her life was his. I am sure she will now just live on for their re-union in a worthier world than ours.

It is in these heartbreaking and intensely personal letters that we see Glen through the eyes of those closest to him. Other letters, from those who knew him as a pilot, speak of a greatly admired and respected comrade. The letter written to George Murrie by Glen's Commanding Officer, Squadron Leader Colin Woodman, is as fine a testimonial as any serviceman might wish for. It was written on 23 September, immediately following the news that A28-55 had been lost, but it would not have been received until several days later. Commanding Officer Woodman offered sympathy to George in 'your grave anxiety', and continued: 'It is considered that both members of the crew must have been killed instantly, but owing to lack of confirmation of this, your son has been posted "missing, believed killed".'[3] He went on to praise Glen, saying that

... he was outstandingly popular throughout the Squadron. He, and F/O Rowlands, his gunner, were admired by all ranks. Glen, who some weeks ago took over a flight in the Squadron, set an excellent example as an Officer and as a Pilot. He, on two occasions, has acted as Commanding Officer of the Squadron during my absence.

In everything he did he was steady and diligent. He was a son of whom you can be completely proud.

A letter from the squadron's chaplain, I.F. Church, written on 9 October and addressed to Lulu, also expressed his sympathy 'in this time of anxiety':

Your son was well known to us all and was thoroughly well liked and admired by the whole squadron. We considered him to be one of the best men we had in the squadron. He entered into the full squadron life and had its welfare well at heart. Personally I found him a great help in my chaplaincy work ...

Naturally such a time must be most difficult for you all, and we up North certainly appreciate this fact and extend to you our sympathy, wishing you a good courage and fortitude ... Meanwhile May God sustain and strengthen you all.

Chapter 21

Coping

In the days following the announcement that Glen was missing, and with the continuing uncertainty over what had actually happened, his brother David volunteered to try to discover the truth. 'I will find out as many particulars as I can,' he wrote home on 29 September, '& will if possible collect his personal belongings.' At that time David was a Flying Officer serving with No. 4 Army Co-operation Squadron, based at Nadzab. He was given leave to visit No. 22 Squadron in Noemfoor, and his own squadron generously arranged air transport for him, saying he could stay in Noemfoor for 'as long as he thought fit'. It was a long journey. He left in the darkness of very early morning, and arrived in the afternoon.

David's next letter home, dated 6 October 1944, made it clear that there were to be no miracles.

Dear Mother Father & Gwenyth,

. . . I arrived back from Glen's squadron this afternoon & found out the facts about poor Glen. I think you may have already received a letter from the C.O. & he has probably told you as much as I know.

As you already know Glen was flying over one of the Kai group of islands & had just completed a barge sweep on the first & was making for the other island at about 200' altitude. The plane covering Glen saw Glen's a/c begin to smoke & then in no time the fire spread quickly & the a/c dived into the sea. The top a/c looked around for a long time afterwards but could not see Glen or his wag F/O Rowlands so Mother I think I am pretty right in saying this & the C.O. of the squadron will bear me out that Glen and his wag were definitely killed in operations. As to the cause of the fire no one will ever know, whether it was caused through ack ack or whether the fault developed in the a/c. The squadron up there has been doing a magnificent job but the job has been a costly one. At about the same time as Glen was killed 4 other crews were also killed within 10 days.

. . . I learnt from the C.O. & also from all the other crews I came in contact with that Glen had done a fine job & that no one was respected more than he was. The ground crews were as upset over the news as were the pilots & gunners as Glen was very popular with them all.

I learnt from the other flight Commander that Glen was well on the way for a decoration & Nancy told me that she had heard he had been recommended. I wouldn't be at all surprised as they said he did an outstanding job.

Now he has gone from us in this world but only for a short time. He was a good Christian & the padre in his squadron admired Glen very much . . .

Please Mother & Father be brave as I know you are & may God help you and comfort you & please don't worry about me Mother. Nancy said you were taking it bravely & that is the greatest comfort you can give me.

There was no hope left. Two families were broken, dreams were shattered, a bright future was lost. Glen's death affected so many people: not just his immediate family, but also his grandmothers Sissy Murrie and Em Murray – the latter now living in a granny flat at Wandeen – his many cousins and aunts and uncles and friends and service colleagues, and, of course, the Priddles.

After reading David's report, Nancy wrote to Lulu, on 12 October,

We have nothing to wait & hope for now but in many ways we are lucky – to know he is not suffering & did not suffer is really the main thing, we who are left will have to bear the pain. And really Mrs Murrie, if we had heard he was a P.O.W. we would have rejoiced, outwardly, but I know how we would have worried about him. I don't think any life would be worth enduring the dreadful things our boys are suffering in Japanese hands & dear old Glen once said, half in fun, but I know he meant it, that he would rather be killed than taken a prisoner by the Japs.

. . . I wonder what happened to the plane to make it blaze, it may have been shot. All day I haven't been able to see anything but the blazing plane diving into the sea.

Bracingly, she continues:

I am going to try & be as bright as I possibly can for Glen did not die for us to be unhappy, he died so that we may be safe & happy so he would not want me to make others lives miserable with my dreadful sadness. In this world

with so many in sorrow we must all try & help each other & see that our glorious boys sacrifices have not been in vain.

Glen will live forever in our hearts & the hearts of hundreds of others & I'm sure there has not been a more loved person in this world . . .

We must just realise now that Glen has been taken from us, and must believe that it is for some higher service, for without that belief our outlook would not be as Glen would want.

For me, it just means finding a new life & I think it will be the Air Force, in that I would feel as if I was getting as near to his unfinished job as I possibly could.

Although letters had flown between Nancy and Lulu and Bertha Priddle, there had been no communication from Sydney, Nancy's father. Nancy had apologised for him, explaining it to Lulu on 2 October:

Daddy is not home yet & we know he will not be writing to you, I know you & I are in his thoughts all the time but he just could not express his thoughts on paper. He wrote to me & we can hardly read the letter, it worried me more than it has comforted me & when the Dear old thing comes home he possibly won't say a word about Glen to me as he just couldn't. He is a wonderful man & everyone loves him but he had a cruel Father which squashed his spirit & if you knew him you would understand why he cannot write to you. In fact even if he wanted to I think we would tell him not to knowing what a strain it would be.

Sydney Priddle did write to Glen's parents, though, and his letter is one of the most touching of the many they received. A very private man, and not in robust physical health, he had taken Glen's death particularly hard. Writing to George and Lulu must have cost him dearly in emotional terms, and makes his letter the more significant. His plan for Glen and Nancy, now shattered, had involved generous practical help to get them on their feet, while still keeping his precious youngest daughter close. Nancy knew about this plan, and in her letter of 2 October she had mentioned it to George and Lulu:

On last Monday & Tuesday while I was in bed with a cold Dad brought a map of "Birangan" down town & showed me where he wanted to split it up & where, if Glen was keen, we would have our home built & the old Darling said, if Glen could not get the money he would sell one of his town houses & build it.

Nancy couldn't wait to tell Glen. All unaware of what had happened, she wrote 'pages & pages' to him on the night before the phone call that would turn her happy world upside down. So Glen never knew of her father's proposal, and Nancy, unable to bear this tangible reminder of the future that was not to be, burned the letter he would never read.

Sydney Priddle's letter, dated 8 October 1944, gave more details.

Dear Mr and Mrs Murrie,

This letter should have been written to you two years ago but up until the present I have always read your letters to Nancy with the greatest of pleasure and now I have to express my deepest sympathy with the loss of your boy or I will say our boy.[1] *He has just enwound himself into our family as one of us, his lovely smile and handsome face was an augury to a perfect man that anyone would be proud to have in their family.*

I was just taking an interest in fixing Nancy up with her share of the place, also June where they would have been only half a mile from each other. We would build a cottage for Nancy and Glen, it would have been on the high tension power where they would have every electric convenience. I was looking forward to having a talk over things with you when you were over and running you out to see the place. I could write a lot of things that Nancy and I had planned for their welfare. So many of these letters must be trying for you at a time like this.

It is far more likely that compassionate, deeply felt letters like Sydney Priddle's touched and comforted George and Lulu rather than adding to their anguish. And they had much need of comfort, for their grief and worry must have been almost unendurable. Glen was dead, killed in the line of duty. David was serving with the RAAF in New Guinea. And Bruce, who was by then a Sub-Lieutenant in the RAN, had recently been involved in a maritime accident and was lucky to escape with his life. On 18 October, twenty-five days after Glen was reported missing, the corvette on which Bruce was serving, HMAS *Geelong*, was sunk in a night collision with an American tanker in the Vitiaz Straits between the New Guinea mainland and New Britain. No lives were lost, as all on board were later picked up by the tanker, but it is conceivable that the Murries could have lost two sons within the month. The *Geelong* was on patrol and escort work when the accident happened. She had been on patrol 'in northern waters' since April 1944, and in that time had covered more than 100,000 miles escorting Allied ships loaded with troops and hundreds of thousands of tons of war supplies.[2]

Bruce's brush with death happened on his twenty-first birthday. When he disembarked near Finschhafen in north-eastern New Guinea he tried to contact David at Nadzab, but was told that his twin was away 'attending to a matter regarding his brother'. David was in fact on compassionate leave at this time. He had returned from Noemfoor on 6 October and was at home with his family in Hazelwood Park. It was the first time Bruce realised that something had happened to Glen, although he was given no details. He too was given leave to return home: coincidentally, he travelled to Adelaide at the same time as David was returning to his squadron. On his way home Bruce managed to contact George and Lulu and for the first time was made aware of what had happened to his older brother. Separated and bereaved, it was a sad birthday for both twins, although the family would have done their best, bravely, to be cheerful.

Nancy, meanwhile, was trying hard to cope. She sought solace in religion, and was impressed by a Baptist couple, Dr and Mrs Young, who were setting up a church in the Forbes district. 'You people and the Youngs are the only Baptists we know,' she had written to Lulu on 2 October, '& I'm sure judging from your two families, your religion is

Nancy with Gwenyth and Bruce at Wandeen in November 1944

a wonderful one.' And she was still making efforts to enlist in one of the services.

In mid-November, having managed to obtain hard-to-get travel permits, Nancy and her mother went on their long-planned visit to Adelaide, staying with the Murries at Wandeen. For Nancy it would be a visit suffused with sadness – very different from that exciting time, fifteen months earlier, when Glen had taken her to meet his family. Her great affection for the Murries, and theirs for her, to some extent filled the terrible void that was Glen's physical absence. For all of them, though, he was in some way still there, conjured up by powerful emotions – unseen, but still present.

Chapter 22

Recognition

There had been an expectation for some time that Glen's outstanding service would be officially recognised. As early as 2 October 1944 Nancy had written to Lulu: 'Don't bank on this as it may be wrong but my cousin's husband saw in a Melbourne paper that Glen had been recommended for a decoration, it is very probable but I'm not thinking about it until we know it is true. You will receive the decoration Mrs Murrie & you certainly deserve more than a medal but I hope it is true for your sake.'

The procedures in place for such recognition moved extremely slowly. Glen's family received 'a Royal message of Condolence' a full ten months after his death, in July 1945.[1] His decoration wasn't confirmed until 7 November 1945, when it was reported that 'the Governor-General (H.R.H. the Duke of Gloucester) has received advice that his Majesty the King has approved of the award for distinguished service in 1st Tactical Air Force in the South-West Pacific area of a mention in dispatch (posthumous) to Flt.-Lt. Glen Inglis Murrie formerly of Hazelwood Park, S.A.'[2]

The citation read:

Flight-Lieutenant Murrie served with No. 22 Squadron for eight months before being posted 'missing, believed killed' on an operational sortie. He showed a sense of responsibility, an understanding of his work, and aircraft, and a capability of leadership of the highest order. He was an outstanding leader in operations and set a high example in courage, determination and ability in attacking his targets.

The award was a source of great pride for both families, but for Bertha Priddle it brought back painful memories:

My dear Mrs Murrie

I did not send you a wire after I heard about the honour bestowed on our darling Glen. But sat down twice to write immediately I heard – and I just Sat – & Sat – I felt I did not want to write. It brought "it" all back with full force.

The Night we got the ring from Mr Murrie – and every word & deed afterwards – oh it is hard to get over this bitter Blow. It has been the blow of my life and I am an old woman . . .

The award certificate, carrying its burden of great pride and equally great sorrow, was sent to George Murrie, who formally acknowledged its receipt on 7 May 1946.

Materially, Glen left behind very little. In his will, dated 28 August 1941, he bequeathed his estate to George as his next of kin. This included deferred pay and the sum of £2 15s 6d in cash, 'paid to the Collector of Public Monies' on 24 September 1944.

His possessions at the time he died are listed by the RAAF in an 'Inventory of Kit' (Caps Flying; Defenders Ear; Ear Pieces Intercommunication; Gauntlets Flying; Goggles

Mask; Scarves Flying; Sox for Boots Flying; Jackets Officers Blue . . . down to Brushes Blacking and Soap Toilet). More immediately poignant are the personal effects, listed separately in a 'Dissection Report' – underwear and pyjamas, swimming trunks, handkerchiefs, his watch, pullovers, a writing case, a safety razor, three books, invasion money, a tin opener.[3] All these items were received by his father 'in perfect condition', as George courteously noted in his acknowledgment letter. However, Glen's logbook was missing, and George was particularly anxious to obtain it. It turned out that the logbook had been retained by the RAAF for security reasons, but with the cessation of hostilities it was released and sent to Glen's parents. It is now kept in the Scotch College archive, as is Glen's white First Eight blazer, which shows the crossed oars and the date 1939 beneath the school crest on the pocket. The day the Scotch Eight won its first Gosse Shield is still counted as one of the proudest in the school's history.

We can never know exactly what happened to A28-55. 'Air operations cause unknown' was the first official statement.[4] Then, on 31 December 1945, the following REPORT ABOUT A CRASHED DOWN AIRPLANE OF THE ALLIES came from 'The Administrator, B.J. Raharoesoen', at Wearlilir in Maluku:

In the month of November 1944 (date unknown) a bomber plane was shot down at the beach near Elaar, it crashed down into the deep sea, and disappeared together with the crew.

The men who shot the plane, were the Japanese Navy, they were guarding there at that beach.

This may well have been Glen's plane: the date is wrong, but memories can be unreliable. An extract from a report by Flight-Lieutenant M.T. O'Shea, dated 1 August 1946, throws a little more light. Under the heading SEARCH FOR MISSING PERSONNEL TANINBAR AND KAI ISLANDS, it gives the following information:

Natives at Toeal reported that an Australian bomber aircraft was shot down in 1944 by a Jap Naval Ack Ack battery, which was guarding the coast in the vicinity of Eter [Elaar?] south-east coast of Little Kai Island. It crashed into the sea and disappeared. The Japs went to the spot in a boat, but nothing was found. This is believed to have been Boston A28-55, as this is the only information received in answer to enquiries regarding it, that could refer to this aircraft.

Although frustratingly inadequate, it is probably as near as we will ever come to an explanation.[5]

Those who loved Glen have no burial place at which to mourn him. His name, one of 442 names of men of the Australian forces with no known grave, is listed on the Ambon Memorial on the Indonesian island of Ambon, close to the south-west coast of Ceram. Along with more than 150 other RAAF servicemen, Glen is 'Commemorated in perpetuity by the Commonwealth War Graves Commission' with the words THEIR NAME LIVETH FOR EVERMORE.[6]

Chapter 23

The Passing Years

Avon Brae continued to play a part in the lives of the Murries. After the war David and Bruce returned to Eden Valley and Barunga Park, the property they had bought in 1940, and which they had planned one day to farm.

While the twins were building a small house on Barunga Park, they lived with my grandparents at Avon Brae, just as Glen and Bruce had done before the war. ('David and Bruce have nearly finished their house & it looks quite well, galv iron & asbestos,' my father wrote to my mother on 14 May 1946, while she was away visiting her family in Melbourne.) During this time David and Elizabeth, my lovely laughing aunt, fell in love. They were married at Scots Church in North Terrace on 11 December 1947. The newlyweds planned to live in the historical old house on Ravenswood, the original homestead of the Matthews estate, but the building, a substantial bluestone with a slate roof, had been unoccupied for many years and required considerable restoration. While it was slowly brought up to habitable standard, David and Elizabeth took over the small house at Barunga Park. Bruce had already left Eden Valley, rejoining the RAN on 30 June 1947 as a Lieutenant.

In those post-war years few people had much money, but life, as in the 1920s, had a reassuring predictability. The war was over, and no more young men were going away to be killed. There was a future to look forward to.

By 1946 my parents were living in the Avon Brae cottage, just a few hundred yards from the main house, and separated from it by a paddock and an orchard. My brother was then three years old, and I was just one. The cottage is the first home I remember: it was small, and old, and homely, and happy. We moved up to the big house when I was four, after my grandparents had relocated to Mount Pleasant. I was nine when my grandfather Will died, in 1955, at the age of seventy-five. I remember this mostly because it was the only time I ever saw my father crying.

David established a dairy farm at Barunga Park, worked hard on restoring the Ravenswood house, and in 1949 became a father. He and Elizabeth named their firstborn son Nicholas Glen.

Bruce was demobilised on 14 September 1948. He married Ann Bruce in 1950 and took up land in Victoria, farming sheep and cattle. When he was in his fifties he moved to the Sunshine Coast, where he still lives.

Gwenyth trained as a nurse at the Royal Adelaide Hospital. In 1953, while visiting the country town of Ardrossan, she met William Lodge, and before long she too was married.

Soon there were sons and daughters, grandchildren, even great-grandchildren.

George Murrie died in 1967 at the age of seventy-three. Lulu outlived him by another thirty years, dying in 1997 just two months short of her hundredth birthday and fifty-three years after the death of her oldest son. George and Lulu are both buried at Snowtown.

Wandeen was sold in 1964, and sold again in the 1990s, and finally demolished. It was replaced by a modern two-storey house. But history is less easily destroyed, and, like Avon Brae, the place where it stood is full of ghosts.

And what of Nancy Priddle?

Nancy didn't give up on her avowed intention, confided to Gwenyth after Glen's death, to do something to make her life more useful. With Bruce's help she found a niche in the RAN Reserve, reporting for duty on 6 February 1945 and giving her occupation as 'home duties'. Two months later her sister Lorraine also joined the RAN, enlisting as a driver. Nancy was assigned to HMAS *Penguin* for training (her job was given as 'assistant writer') and passed her typing test on 7 February. She was transferred to HMAS *Kuttabul*, then to the *Lonsdale* and the *Torrens*. But the war was nearly over now, and Nancy's contribution came to an end in July 1946.[1]

While Nancy was serving in the navy, her cherished 'old Darling' father Sydney died suddenly on 23 June 1946, aged only sixty-nine. Bertha Priddle continued to live at East Anglia. Like Lulu Murrie, she outlived her husband by many years, dying on 14 October 1974.

Nancy was only just twenty-one when Glen died, and she had her whole life ahead of her. Slowly she began to live again, to go out, to make an effort. She had many friends. And she did find happiness. On 12 June 1948 she married Greville Griffith, formerly a Forbes man, at Holy Trinity Anglican Church, Grenfell. She was attended by her sister June, and 'little Jill', who was now four and a half years old.

After the wedding, according to *Truth* in its 'Roundabout' page of social gossip (20 June 1948), a 'very cheery reception was held at the C.W.A. Cottage, Grenfell', where Nancy had once stolen the show as a two-year-old Balloon Girl.

Greville Griffith had recently bought a property at Manildra, and it was here that he and Nancy made their first home. They had three sons and continued to live in the district, later moving to another property, Victoria Park.

Lorraine's wedding to Eric Forbes was announced in the *Forbes Advocate* on 31 March 1953. The last of the Priddle sisters to marry, she had no children herself but was a much-loved aunt, 'Rainy', to her nephews and nieces.

Nancy threw herself wholeheartedly into marriage and motherhood. Determined to put the sorrows of the past behind her, she gave Gwenyth the album that held her treasured photographs and mementoes of Glen. It was her family that was important to her now.

The worn and tattered album is a treasure-house of memories for Glen's family, as it once was for Nancy herself. Each photograph, each tiny memento, is a cherished fragment of Glen himself – the son, the brother, the fiancé, the pilot.

At the back of the album Nancy has pasted souvenirs of happy gatherings: the jokey menu for a RAAF passing-out dinner, invitations to service dances and cocktail parties. The invitations are formally worded, typeset in the standard copperplate, printed on thin card. In difficult times it's vital that appearances be kept up, and the familiar social conventions are solid and comforting.

The last few pages comprise a sort of scrapbook. Here, stuck down edge to edge, are clippings from newspapers, printed signposts to a past life. Few are dated, and, as with the photographs that fill the rest of the album, there is no particular chronology. There are engagement announcements – six of them, from different publications – and chatty reports from social notes. There are news stories. The largest clipping, from the Sydney *Sun* of 26 August 1944, bears the bold headline: 'Merciless Pounding of Jap Shipping and Bases in Dutch N.G.'. Underneath it, we read:

*In Bostons, Kittyhawks and Beaufighters, Australians are gradually forcing Japan to the doubtful safety of tiny bays and harbours. They are also smashing vital shore installations . . . Bostons lobbed eight bombs among buildings on the Klamono oilfield, south of Sorong, causing extensive damage . . . An aircraft piloted by Flight-Lieutenant G. Murray [*sic*] (S.A.) accurately bombed buildings at a possible oil-well at the junction of the Klasapat and Klasapo rivers, destroying two structures and causing fires.*

Klamono. Sorong. Klasapat. Klasapo. Once they were strategically important to winning the war. Today they are forgotten by almost everybody, nothing but exotic names on fragile, yellowing newsprint.

Another news clipping graphically describes, but doesn't show, a photograph depicting the beheading of an Australian serviceman, at the time thought to be Bill Newton from No. 22 Squadron but later identified as an AIF Special Operations sergeant, Len Siffleet.[2] (*This grim picture of death in the presence of a circle of grinning Japanese was taken from the body of a dead Jap . . . Dressed in a short-sleeved shirt and jackboots, a scrawny-armed bespectacled Jap stands over the victim with sword upraised.*) Nancy may have kept this clipping as a bleakly consoling reminder that Glen had at least escaped this brutal fate. On the same page she has pasted a Japanese 'Tien Cent' banknote and a newspaper photograph headed 'Allies Honour Men Who Gave Their Lives': *On Noemfoor Island an American paratrooper and an Australian airman carry the colors into an Allied cemetery during a memorial service for men killed in action on the island.* There is no date. Below it, also undated, is another newspaper photograph headed 'Aussies On The Job' and captioned *RAAF Men: Members of a Boston Bomber Squadron which, from an island base, is cleaning up remnants of the Japanese task force in the Vogelkop Peninsula, Dutch New Guinea.* Glen isn't in the photograph. One of the men, perched above the propeller of a Boston, is Flying Officer Dargan McKenzie.

Several media reports of Glen's death have been pasted into the album – with what renewed sorrow, who can guess? His blurred portrait appears beneath the heading 'Private Casualty Advices' in the Adelaide *Advertiser* (29 September 1944) and in a more personal report for a local newspaper, probably the *Grenfell Record*, which would be read by many who knew the Priddles: *Distressing news was received yesterday by Miss Nancy Priddle to the effect that her fiance, Flight-Lieutenant Glen Murrie, failed to return to his base in his Boston Bomber on Saturday . . .* On the same album page, in tiny type, is an official RAAF List, most likely from one of the major newspapers. Glen's name is listed under 'Previously Reported Missing, Now Presumed Dead'. A similarly modest notice ('Canberra, November 7') is headed 'Posthumous Award to S.A. Airman'.

A newspaper sketch in cartoon style shows a 'Douglas A-20 (Boston) Attack Bomber', coloured bright green, flying over hectic pink clouds.

And there are poems. Nancy has carefully typed out 'An Airman's Prayer' by Sergeant Observer H.R. (Hugh) Brodie, RAAF: *But this I pray – be at my side/ When death is drawing through the sky/ Almighty God who also died/ Teach me the way that I should die.*[3] Beside it, cut from a newspaper, is 'Wings', by Freda Vines, a Western Australian writer and poet whose first husband, also a Flight-Lieutenant in the RAAF, was killed in January 1945:

My love has wings . . . swift wings to lift him far
Into the blue, leaving the world behind.
Leaving the world, to reach and touch a star,
Climbing the secret pathways of the wind.
White seas of cloud, morning and sunsets gold,
Starlight and day; freedom of the skies
Are his, to share with other men who hold
The dawn of far horizons in their eyes . . .
Who, light of heart, go climbing to the sun,
The engines' song an echo to their mirth,
Exulting in the glory they have won
Like Gods, a little careless of the earth.

My love has wings. Yet I am well content
To earthbound be, watching the bombers sweep
Seaward like drowsy bees drugged with the scent
Of clover from some summer pastures deep.
My love has wings. But when we have to part,
Shall I not weep, with happiness in pawn?
Ah no! How should I, when my eager heart
Has wings to fly beside him to the dawn![4]

It is poetry drenched in romantic sentiment, thick with yearning. To a young girl – and Nancy was so very young – faced suddenly with the agony of bereavement, it may have offered some small comfort by mirroring, however imperfectly, what was in her own heart. Seen through the poem's heightened imagery, the pilot is a glorious, carefree being who soars high above the ruck of ordinary earth-bound men. Death, in that context, is free from pain and terror, blood and burning.

Nancy kept in touch with Glen's family all her life. On at least a couple of occasions George and Lulu Murrie stayed with her and her family at Victoria Park. Nancy's oldest son, Sydney, remembers them from the mid-1950s, vividly recalling 'Mr Murrie' as a kind and gentle man, and 'the very first man I ever met with one leg!'. Not a year went past without the exchange of a card or a letter. Against all the odds, and as a tribute to the character of both Nancy and the Murries, their relationship lasted through births and deaths, widowhood and illness. Gwenyth, with whom Nancy had a particularly strong bond, visited her only weeks before she died.

I have seen a photograph of Nancy in old age. When the Driftway Public School held a big reunion in 2013, she was feted as one of the original class of 1928. There she is, on the front page of the *Grenfell Record* dated 3 May 2013. 'Memories Come Drifting Back', says the headline. And underneath the photo of three elderly people sitting in the back of a bus, the caption reads: *Three of the oldest, if not the oldest, original Driftway School pupils at the* *site of the old school during a tour that was part of last weekend's Driftway School Reunion in Grenfell were (l/r) Ron Lamkin, Nancy Griffiths [*sic*] (nee Priddle) and Noel Hunter.*

Nancy's trim figure has broadened with age and child-bearing, and her face has the gentle questing look you sometimes see in an older woman, as if she can't quite believe that she has reached the age she certainly is, and wonders how it happened. But I feel that I know her a little now, and she is indisputably still Nancy. Grey-haired and wearing glasses, she looks neat and pretty in her warm cherry-pink cardigan and pale lilac blouse with a peter pan collar.

It can't have been long after this photo was taken that Nancy moved into a nursing home. Her memory was beginning to slip away, and her health was failing. But as her recent memories faded, her recall of the past became stronger. Moving towards the end of her life, she began to speak more openly of Glen. The joy of her first love, and the tragedy of its ending, was as clear and vivid as ever.

And what was in Glen's mind all those years ago, just before his plane erupted in flames? Perhaps he was thinking of the last time he saw his Nancy, waving, waving as the train took him further and further away from her. Perhaps his last complete memory was of her eager, beloved face.

Chapter 24

Afterthoughts

I go for a walk every morning. As I try to keep up a good pace, I'm intensely aware of being alive: muscles stretch and contract, heart pumps, lungs heave in and out. Cells replicate, hair and nails grow. Blood warms me, sweat films my skin. Although sometimes it falters, the body machine is still working.

This morning, as I walk, I think of Glen.

I tend to live with the characters I am writing about, whether they are real or fictional, and when I have finished writing I have a sense of loss. Over many months Glen has become my chief imaginary companion, although I'm not sure of the context. It's strange, this one-sided connection. He is more than the clinical-sounding 'second cousin once removed' that is his true relationship to me. More than just my uncle's brother. He exists, now and for always, in my mind.

I'm aware that there are huge gaps in my reconstruction of his life. In the absence of relevant source material, I have tried to fill some of those gaps with my imagination, and sometimes I may be uncomfortably wide of the mark. And even when I am on surer ground, I realise that the most exhaustive compilation of facts and details and recollections has its limitations. The man himself, the real flesh-and-blood person, can only truly be known by those who knew and loved him.

Still (I tell myself), I have managed to discover quite a lot.

I know what Glen looks like. *Looked* like. He had a good face, even a handsome one. It was the sort of face you'd trust. He had an attractive smile, but he was a bit shy, a bit serious, so maybe he didn't smile often. I expect that his voice was very like my uncle's voice: deep, with an accent that used to be described (in the days when news-readers were expected to speak with an English plum) as 'educated Australian'.

From his actions, and from the comments of others, I know something of his character. *Excellent*, my uncle said. *Decent*, a word seldom used these days, also comes to mind. *Steady. Loyal. Kind. Courageous. Modest. High-achieving.* Heartbreakingly, *A son of whom you can be completely proud.* Everything he did, whether it was playing the piano or rowing a race or flying a Boston Bomber, he did to the best of his ability.

I know what he wasn't. He wasn't a dare-devil. He wasn't a show-off. He wasn't a coward. He wasn't selfish, or shallow, or treacherous, or faithless.

He wasn't outstandingly talented, or brilliantly witty, or deeply intellectual, either. You'd probably find him reading *Popular Mechanics* or magazines on farming practice rather than Dickens. At school he would have been somewhere in the top half of the class. He was intelligent, logical, practical, clear-headed.

I suspect that he was a romantic, in the way of many young men who might not admit, even to themselves, that they have a softer, more sensitive side. I imagine him at Avon Brae, playing the old upright piano that one day I too would play. I imagine him, later, amazed by the extraordinary happiness of being in love, and being loved in return.

He offered himself for war service because like so many of his contemporaries, including his brothers, he believed it was the right thing to do, the *honourable* thing to do. (In wartime the principle of patriotic duty is frequently and stirringly evoked by public figures and heads of state, and of course it is mainly young men they target.) Nor did he lack courage. It was part of his character and also part of his heritage, the example set by the hardy Scottish and English men and women from whom he was descended.

Religious faith was central to Glen's life in a way that many of today's younger generation might find difficult to understand. It's fashionable nowadays to decry those who believe in a higher being, although I imagine that during the perils of war many an atheist has offered up the occasional fervent prayer. Devoutness, like overt patriotism, is partly a generational thing. I recall the words of my grandfather, grieving the loss of his father: *I know that the Lord will give you all that is good for you, if you fear him and do your best.*

Glen was only twenty-two when he died, but he was no longer a boy. He never experienced the cheerful hedonism of today's youth, or its particular challenges, or its uncertainty. Almost from the moment of leaving school, he had taken on adult responsibilities. His two great loves were flying and the land, but his personal ambition was in effect to re-create the sort of life his parents had – to have a successful marriage, a comfortable home, and a family.

His wartime service done, he would have turned all his energies to achieving these goals, with Nancy by his side. Together they would have built up a thriving rural property, and over the years he would have established the almost visceral connection with the earth that is granted to a farmer and stays with him all his life. But Glen never became the farmer he so dearly wanted to be. The home he was to have shared with Nancy was never built. Their children were never born.

Glen loved the freedom of flight, the sheer excitement of it. Each bombing mission was joy and dread combined: life poised on a knife's edge. Chance after chance taken, each freighted with the possibility of disaster.

Suddenly, on 23 September 1944, the odds were no longer in his favour.

What happened on that day turned the course of many lives. Nothing could bring Glen back, but the tragedy of his death also allowed the possibility, in time, of unexpected happiness, and the existence of generations that otherwise would not have been born. Life goes on, despite everything, and wars do end, although their impact remains.

We can only imagine what might have been if A28-55 had made it back to base. All we have is reality, and memories. Memories that must continue to honour the sacrifice of brave lives so willingly offered, so cruelly cut short.

Appendix

Scotch College Speech Night, 19 December 1939

The Scotch College Speech Night for 1939, Glen's final year at the school, was reported in its entirety in the *Advertiser* on 20 December 1939. The event was attended by the State Governor, Sir Malcolm Barclay-Harvey, who in his opening speech reminded the audience that the school had been established 'in memory of the men who had gone forth to the Great War, when it was hoped they would not see war again in their time'. He feared that the present struggle would be a long and bitter one, but felt that 'if needs be the [Scotch] boys would be none the less men than those who had gone before them'.

The chairman of the school council, Mr G.C. Ligertwood, took up the same theme, finishing his address by saying: 'Old scholars of the school had already shown their loyalty, and a number of them had marched away in the Second A.I.F. *(applause)*. Others were getting ready to join up as soon as the Commonwealth Government told them that their services were needed. Every school in the State, both private and State, had shown that the youth of South Australia, and of Australia, stood solidly behind the Government in its efforts for freedom, and the Government could rely on the old scholars of Scotch College to do their bit when the time came.'

The headmaster, Mr Norm Gratton, then gave a lengthy speech in which he summarised the school's successes (including the winning of the Gosse Shield), gave congratulations to all prize-winners, and recorded his gratitude to teachers and benefactors. His concluding comments are worth reporting more fully:

On the occasion of my first annual report, delivered from this platform 21 years ago, in December, 1919, we rejoiced that the frightful war of 1914–1918 was ended, and we confidently looked forward to the incalculable joys of a permanent peace. But after the comparatively brief period of 21 years, the hopes of 1919 have been seriously shattered, and we again find ourselves committed to a major war, the effects of which, both on individuals and on nations, no one can presume to predict. This war must affect very seriously the expected course of life of these, and thousands of other boys. Consequently, schools have to face the added problem of training boys to understand, and live in, a future environment, which cannot but be very problematic . . .

We regret the necessity of saying 'good-bye' to a number of boys tonight, and so breaking what has been a stimulating and delightful association, but we look forward with pleasure to meeting them, from now on, on a more intimate footing. The school will always be very glad to see them and rejoice with them in their successes and sympathise with them in their disappointments.

I would say to these boys, in the words of Newbolt, that we have tried to inspire them

To set the cause above renown,
To love the game beyond the prize,
To honour, while you strike him down,
The foe that comes with fearless eyes;
To count the life of battle good,
And dear the land that gave you birth,
And dearer yet the brotherhood
That binds the brave of all the earth.[1]

and we are sure that, in success or in failure, they will bravely strive to live up to these ideals. And now, may I wish you all a very happy Christmas season, and express the hope that, during 1940, peace may be more evident than seems possible at present.[2]

Chapter Notes

All through the book I have used imperial measurements. My sources invariably give the measurements in use at the time, and my initial attempts at metrication were soon abandoned. (A 0.5-inch machine-gun is a 0.5-inch machine-gun, not a 12.7-mm machine-gun.)

Chapter 1: Finding

1 The *Josephine* books were written by an English writer for children, Mrs H.C. Cradock, and illustrated by Honor C. Appleton. The first title, *Josephine and her Dolls*, was published in 1915.

2 The Eden Valley opens into the Barossa Valley, and like the Barossa it was settled by a mix of British and German immigrants. Most of the Germans were Lutherans from Silesia (Prussia) escaping religious persecution in their homeland. At Eden Valley Primary School in the 1950s, the children, all of us wholly Australian, were about half of British and half of German descent.

The history of Eden Valley is well recorded in Reg Butler's comprehensive book *The Quiet Waters By: The Mount Pleasant District 1843–1993*, published by the District Council of Mount Pleasant in 1993.

3 The Voluntary Aid Detachment (VAD) was an organisation founded in England in 1909 by the Red Cross and the Order of St John. Its members consisted almost entirely of women volunteers who in wartime provided basic domestic and nursing

services, mainly in hospitals and convalescent homes. They were given some medical training, but were not qualified nurses.

Chapter 2: Avon Brae

1 To my continuing astonishment, 'Avon Brae' is now a wine label.

2 I have the specification for the original building, a four-roomed house and passage, handwritten on two sheets of lined foolscap. It is dated 2 August 1918 and signed by the builder, Ad Rohrlach. The agreed cost of the build was £300. A room built at right angles to the main house was added later.

Chapter 3: 2000 and Beyond

1 A detailed history of the Matthews estate, once by far the biggest land-holding in the Eden Valley area, can be found in Reg Butler's *The Quiet Waters By*.

Chapter 4: Families

1 Glen Turret still exists, and the old homestead looks much the same as it appears in my painting.

2 The family tree that helped me to make sense of our extended family was given to me by my uncle David Murrie. It is a complicated document, four A4 sheets sticky-taped together. For this book I have abbreviated and simplified it, leaving out many individual names and omitting the post-war generation and beyond (pages viii–ix).

3 For this chapter I made use of two family histories: *The Vigar Family: Pioneers in Australia 1828–1978*, by Robert T. Vigar (Peacock Publications, Adelaide, 1979) and *A Mile of Shannon*, compiled by Margaret (Murray) Vowles (Frankston, Victoria, 1990). Information about the Murrays of Glen Turret can also be found in *Valley of Smithys, Schools & Spires: Moculta 1842–1942* by Reg S. Munchenberg, published in 1982 by the Moculta Centenary Book Committee.

An interesting pictorial archive, including portraits of Pulteney and Elizabeth Murray and several historical photographs of Glen Turret, is on the South Australian Library's website at http://collections.slsa.sa.gov.au/resource/B+41432.

4 A number of websites give details of shipping from Great Britain in the nineteenth century, together with comprehensive passenger lists of immigrants to South Australia. One I found helpful was http://www.theshipslist.com/ships/australia/SAassistedindex.shtml.

5 My father once owned the photograph of Elizabeth Murray taken either before or after she made this historic flight. The actual photograph has since disappeared, but it has been reproduced in *The Vigar Family*, page 43.

Chapter 5: Searching

1 I obtained most of the information in this chapter by delving into the National Library of Australia's marvellous and indispensable Trove archive of digitised Australian newspapers.

2 George Inglis died on 26 February 1914. His obituary appeared in the *Register*, 27 February 1914.

3 Peter Murrie's death in South Africa was reported in the *Advertiser*, 14 June 1901.

4 George Murrie's accident was reported in the *Adelaide Chronicle*, 14 October 1905.

5 Eliza Inglis's eighty-fifth birthday was marked by lengthy articles in both the *Register* on 3 June 1925 and the Adelaide *Observer* three days later. Her ninetieth birthday was reported in the *News* on 27 March 1930. Her obituary appeared in the *News*, 13 January 1931.

6 Most of my information about Lulu Murrie's early life and marriage comes from Lulu herself. On 4 May 1982 she was interviewed by Margaret Preiss for the Australia 1938 Oral History Project as research for the book *Australians 1938*, from the series *Australians, a historical library*. The resulting sound recording is available on a 90-minute cassette held by the State Library of South Australia (Bib ID 953637).

7 Lulu Murrie made this comment about the role of the mother in response to her interviewer asking her how she saw the 'typical Australian male' and 'typical Australian female'.

Chapter 6: Wandeen

1 Details about the birth of the babies were given to me by my uncle. Descriptions of the Murrie family's home and their daily life are based on information in Lulu Murrie's interview tape, State Library of South Australia (Bib ID 953637).

2 Lulu says in her interview that the children read 'books like *Little Lord Fauntleroy* and *Cole's Funny Picture Book*'. Now with a status somewhere between a classic and a curio, *Cole's Funny Picture Book* was first self-published in 1879 by Edward Cole, owner of Cole's Book Arcade in Melbourne. It was frequently reprinted and has sold over a million copies. The sweet, sentimental, highly moral novel *Little Lord Fauntleroy*, by Frances Hodgson Burnett, was first published in 1886 and is still in print.

Bruce Murrie told me a fascinating story related to a children's book that had once belonged to Glen. A little while ago a woman named Vivienne McGrath bought an old copy of *Johnny Bear*, by Ernest Thompson Seton, from a second-hand bookshop in Samford, Queensland. Some time later, when she opened the book and saw Glen's name and address written on the flyleaf, she decided to see if she could find him, or any existing relatives. Unbelievably, the day she opened the book was 7 March, Glen's birthday. After some diligent research she managed to get in touch with Bruce and gave the book to him. *Johnny Bear* was an eighth-birthday present to Glen from Lulu, and it was she who had inscribed it with his name and address, and the date 7/3/30.

Chapter 7: Forbes, New South Wales

1 The 'Hop Back to Grenfell' festival was described at length in an article published in the *Sydney Morning Herald* on 20 March 1924. 'The baby show had many entries, the winner being Nancy Priddle (for girl) and Kenneth Flinn (for boy). The best-looking school boy was Bruce Armstrong, and school girl, Beatrice McLeod.'

2 The photograph of eight-month-old Nancy and her mother appeared in the *Sydney Mail*, 30 April 1924.

3 The fancy-dress balls I have described were reported in the *Grenfell Record and Lachlan District Advertiser* (henceforth referred to as just the *Grenfell Record*) on 23 March 1925 and 13 September 1928.

4 Information about the Driftway School, and the photo of its first students, appear in the Facebook page set up in 2013 by the Driftway Public School Reunion Committee: https://www.facebook.com/driftwayreunion2013.

5 The Plain and Fancy Dress Ball was reported in the *Grenfell Record* on 20 October 1932. 'As a result of the effort the school fund [benefited] to the extent of £5 10s.'

6 The 1932 Christmas party was reported in the *Grenfell Record* on 12 December 1932.

7 Details of the Driftway School Annual Picnic and Sports Day appeared in the *Grenfell Record* on 16 October 1933. Events included the usual flat races and three-legged races for different age groups, along with (for adults) a Married Ladies' Race, a Sweethearts' Race, and Hitting Tennis Ball through Motor Tyre.

8 The 1933 Christmas Tree and Break-up Party and prize-giving were described in the *Grenfell Record* on 14 December 1933.

9 Nancy's first prize for her garden plot was reported in the *Grenfell Record* on 1 October 1934; the examination results appeared on 29 November 1934.

Chapter 8: Gathering Clouds

1 Air Commodore Sir Charles Kingsford Smith, piloting the *Lady Southern Cross*, disappeared with his co-pilot over the Andaman Sea early in the morning of 8 November 1935. On 11 November an article in the *Advertiser* said of the flying ace that he . . .

possessed in a supreme degree certain qualities of skill, intrepidity, and endurance, in consideration of which every Australian was proud to be called his fellow-countryman . . . His almost unrivalled popularity is indicative of man's ineradicable fondness for romantic daring. This instinctive feeling for heroism, which produced and elaborated the ancient stories of knight errantry, has survived every change in our manners and social environment; and the present generation has been willing to substitute for the Lancelots and Galahads of fable, lumbering through life on horseback and in heavy armor, the knights of the air, whose steeds roar above the clouds at speeds which a few years ago would have been deemed incredible, and whose meteoric pilgrimages have so contracted the earth that even its greatest distances now seem almost trifling.

Chapter 9: Head of the River

1 My schoolboy father's bravery was reported in several newspapers, including the *Sydney Morning Herald*, 18 November 1931, and the *Chronicle*, 19 November 1931. He also appears in a group photograph of those receiving awards from the Royal Humane Society of Australia (*Chronicle*, 25 August 1932).

2 A great deal of historical information about Mitcham can be found in the Mitcham Council's walking guide at http://www.mitchamcouncil.sa.gov.au/webdata/resources/files/Mitcham_Village_Walk_Brochure.pdf.

3 Discussions of the form shown by the schools involved, and reports on the Head of the River itself, have been taken from various newspapers. The *News* reported on the lead-up to the race on 18 April 1939, and articles by 'our Rowing Correspondent' appeared in the *Advertiser* on 18, 21 and 22 April 1939 ('Record Crowds Expected'). The results of the race were reported only hours after its conclusion in the *Mail* (by 'Swivel') on 22 April, and by the *Advertiser* and the *News* on 24 April 1939. Descriptions of the social and fashion scene, down to the last hat feather, appeared in the *Mail* ('Fashions and Cheers at Head of River') on 22 April 1939.

Chapter 10: Jackeroos

1 Information about my father's time in the RAAF is contained in his service record, National Archives of Australia: A9301, 26194, Vigar, L.W.S.

2 Details from the *Advertiser* dated 17 February 1940.

3 With the RAF critically understaffed when war broke out, the British Government devised a plan to train 50,000 air crew annually, the number to be made up of recruits from each of the British dominions. On 17 December 1939 an agreement was signed in Ottawa, Canada, by which Australia agreed to provide 28,000 trained air crew over three years, the intention being that they would serve with the RAF. The scheme was known in Australia as the Empire Air Training Scheme. More information is available on the Australian War Memorial website at https://www.awm.gov.au/encyclopedia/raaf/eats.
4 During the First World War, in a sweeping obliteration of Germanic place-names, the Rhine was re-named the Marne, but locally the old name stuck.

Chapter 11: The Right Decision

1 A complete list of those who purchased sections of the Matthews Estate in 1940 appears in Reg Butler's *The Quiet Waters By*, pp. 548–49. The buyers of Section 543 and part of Section 544 have been incorrectly given in the book as 'Mary Murray & George Norrie'. 'Norrie' should be 'Murrie'.

Chapter 12: Life on the Land

1 This listing of a farmer's tasks throughout the year became the basis for my children's picture book *A Year on Our Farm* (Omnibus Books, 2002). Sadly, my father died long before the book was published.

Chapter 13: Nineteen

1 For this chapter, and throughout the rest of the book, I have referred extensively to Glen's service record, National Archives of Australia: A9300, Murrie, G.I.
2 Information about the Initial Training Schools, and other training schools established as part of the Empire Air Training Scheme, can be found at https://en.wikipedia.org/wiki/List_of_British_Commonwealth_Air_Training_Plan_facilities_in_Australia and on the Australian War Memorial website at https://www.awm.gov.au/encyclopedia/raaf/eats.

3 The story of Mount Breckan is outlined at https://en.wikipedia.org/wiki/Mount_Breckan.

Chapter 14: Western Junction

1 When writing about Glen's training at Western Junction I found a great deal of helpful background information in *Battle Order 204: A Bomber Pilot's Story*, by Christobel Mattingley (Allen & Unwin, 2007). This book is a biography of Christobel's husband, David, who trained at Western Junction in 1942 and later flew Lancaster bombers over Europe.

2 According to Glen's logbook, the name of his instructor is Flying Officer Scascighini. (Perhaps he was known affectionately as 'Scasgilini' by his pupils?)

Chapter 15: Flying Solo

1 A Gestetner copy of the typewritten Sequence of Instruction is pasted into Glen's logbook.

2 A great deal of information about the Wirraway can be found at https://www.airforce.gov.au/raafmuseum/research/aircraft/series2/A20.htm and https://en.wikipedia.org/wiki/CAC_Wirraway#Specifications_.28CAC_Wirraway.29.

3 The Second World War is the background to Glen's story, not the story itself. I have gone to various articles in Wikipedia for basic information about the progress of the war in the Pacific and the Japanese raids on Darwin.

4 Information about Parkes and the Empire Air Training Scheme can be found at http://en.wikipedia.org/wiki/RAAF_Station_Parkes.

Chapter 16: Nancy

1 A brief description of June's wedding to Victor Bradford appears in the *Grenfell Record* of 30 April 1942. It was quite a small wedding, as so many were in those war years, but among the guests were 'three soldier comrades of the bridegroom from abroad'.

2 An account of rationing in Australia during the Second World War can be found on the Australian War Memorial website at https://www.awm.gov.au/encyclopedia/homefront/rationing.

Chapter 17: Engagements and a Wedding

1 Regarding the Japanese defeat of the British in Singapore, Wikipedia has come to my rescue yet again. Two useful sites to which I referred are https://en.wikipedia.org/wiki/Battle_of_Singapore and https://en.wikipedia.org/wiki/Japanese_occupation_of_Singapore.

2 The lines come from Laurence Binyon's poem, 'For the Fallen', first published in *The Times* on 21 September 1914. It is best known for the verse traditionally repeated on every Anzac Day:

They shall grow not old, as we that are left grow old:
Age shall not weary them, nor the years condemn.
At the going down of the sun and in the morning
We will remember them.

3 An auctioneer's notice in the *Grenfell Record* for 13 March 1941 advertises 'a clearing sale [on] account [of] Mr S. Priddle on Wednesday 2nd April when they will sell sheep, cattle, horses, machinery, furniture, etc.' Birangan was leased until 1946, after which the lease (for seven years) was taken up by June and Vic Bradford.

4 This album is now in the possession of Gwenyth Lodge.

5 From the report in the *Sydney Morning Herald* on the opening of the club, 25 August 1943.

6 The statement is contained in Glen's logbook.

7 For this description of the last time Nancy saw Glen, I am indebted to Nancy's daughter-in-law Janet Griffith, to whom Nancy told the story.

Chapter 18: No. 22 Squadron

1 In writing about the history of No. 22 Squadron, I have drawn on https://en.wikipedia.org/wiki/No._22_Squadron_RAAF; on the Australian War Memorial website https://www.awm.gov.au/unit/U59385; and on the website of the No. 22 (City of Sydney)

Squadron Association, http://www.22squadronassociation.org.au.

2 There are several useful sources of information about Boston Bombers, including the RAAF Museum website http://www.airforce.gov.au/raafmuseum/exhibitions/tech_hang/boston.htm, and ADF-SERIALS: Australian & New Zealand Military Aircraft Serials & History, RAAF A28 Douglas DB-7B, A-20A, A-20C & A20G Boston, http://www.adf-serials.com.au/2a28.htm. Stewart Wilson's *Boston, Mitchell & Liberator in Australian Service* (Aerospace Publications, Weston Creek, ACT, 1992) is another excellent resource.

3 A detailed description of the Battle of the Bismarck Sea can be found at https://en.wikipedia.org/wiki/Battle_of_the_Bismarck_Sea. A more succinct account appears on the Australian War Memorial website https://www.awm.gov.au/talks-speeches/battle-of-bismarck-sea.

4 Much has been written about Flight-Lieutenant Bill Newton, including a biography, *Bill Newton V.C.: The Short Life of a RAAF Hero*, by Mark Weate (Australian Military History Publications, 1999).

5 Details of Glen's first missions are taken from the Historical Data section of the No. 22 Squadron Association's website, http://www.22squadronassociation.org.au, which contains a complete record of all operations flown by the squadron.

6 For information about Noemfoor I went to a US Army website history ('The War in the Pacific: The Approach to the Philippines') written by Robert Ross Smith: Chapter XVII, 'Operations on Noemfoor Island', http://www.ibiblio.org/hyperwar/USA/USA-P-Approach/USA-P-Approach-17.html.

7 In its photographic archive https://www.awm.gov.au/collection/photographs the Australian War Memorial has a collection of photographs of No. 22 Squadron at Noemfoor. Most were taken around August 1944.

Chapter 19: On Active Service

1 All descriptions of operations carried out by Glen and others are taken from the No. 22 Squadron Association's Historical Data, http://www.22squadronassociation.org.au.

2 The interviews relating to this accident (compiled and prepared by Glen, and signed off after his death by his Commanding Officer, Colin Woodman), are contained in Flying Officer James Davidson's casualty file, National Archives of Australia: A705, 166/9/387, Davidson, J.E.
3 Information taken from ADF-SERIALS: Australian & New Zealand Military Aircraft Serials & History, http://www.adf-serials.com.au/2a28.htm.
4 This site, http://www.adf-serials.com.au/2a28.htm, also contains a detailed history of every Boston used by the RAAF. The list clearly indicates some of the problems involved with the aircraft.
5 The official records of the downing of A28-55 are contained in Glen's casualty file, National Archives of Australia: A705, 166/28/413, Murrie, G.I.

Chapter 20: Missing

1 The telegram sent to Glen's family no longer exists, but a carbon copy typescript is contained in Glen's casualty file.
2 There is a copy of this official memorandum in Glen's casualty file.
3 Copies of the personally signed letters from Commanding Officer Colin Woodman and Chaplain I.F. Church are in Glen's casualty file. There are two versions of the letter from CO Woodman. The first says that Glen is 'missing presumed killed'. On the advice of No. 5 Base Personnel Staff Office (BPSO), to which all letters of condolence were sent for censorship, this statement was later amended to read 'missing believed killed'. This decision was upheld by Group Captain Walker, Staff Office Administration, No. 10 (Operational) Group. On 6 October 1944, in a memo to No. 5 BPSO, he wrote: 'In the circumstances, it would be unfair to hold out any hope of survival to the relatives . . . It is agreed that the Commanding Officer should have used the words "missing believed killed" instead of "missing presumed killed", because of the legal implications of the word "presumed".'

Chapter 21: Coping

1 *This letter should have been written to you two years ago . . .* Sydney Priddle is probably making a reference to the end of 1942, when Nancy and Glen became engaged.
2 The sinking of HMAS *Geelong* was reported in several Australian newspapers, including the *Sydney Morning Herald* on 28 October 1944.

Chapter 22: Recognition

1 A cover sheet on Glen's casualty file contains the words: 'Considered an appropriate case for the issue of a Royal message of Condolence.' This message was recorded as having been sent to George Murrie on 19 July 1945.
2 Glen's Mention in Despatches was reported in both the *Canberra Times* and the *Advertiser* on 8 November 1945. A carbon copy typescript of the citation is also contained in Glen's service record.
3 As routine procedure, the Dissection Report was always prepared by friends of the dead serviceman so that his possessions could be vetted (and, if necessary, 'cleaned up') before being sent to his family.
4 This assessment is made in a confidential Cypher Message, dated 25 September 1944, from No. 5 Base Personnel Staff Office to RAAF Headquarters, Northern Command, and is now in Glen's casualty file.
5 The note from B.J. Raharoesoen and the extract from Flight-Lieutenant O'Shea's report are in Glen's casualty file.
6 Details obtained from the Commonwealth War Graves Commission, http://www.cwgc.org.

Chapter 23: The Passing Years

1 Nancy's time in the Royal Australian Naval Reserve is documented in her service record held by the National Archives of Australia: NAA: A6770, Priddle, N. K.
2 A biography of Len Siffleet can be found on the Australian War Memorial website, https://www.awm.gov.au/people/P10676744.
3 'An Airman's Prayer', one of the best loved of all war poems, is often quoted at memorial services. Its author, Melbourne

schoolteacher Hugh Brodie, served with No. 460 Squadron, RAAF, attached to the RAF. He was killed along with the rest of his crew when their Wellington bomber disappeared over Germany in July 1942. http://aircrewremembered.com/levitus-solomon.html.

4 Freda Vines (1916–2000) wrote romantic short stories, radio plays and poetry. Her best known work, *The Maker of Music: A Story of the RAAF* (1944), is a long narrative poem about the pilot and crew of a Beaufort Bomber. I cannot find a source for 'Wings', but suspect that it was first published in a Western Australian newspaper, probably before the death of Vines' pilot husband in 1945.

Appendix: Scotch College Speech Night, 19 December 1939

1 The lines quoted are from 'Clifton Chapel', by the English poet Sir Henry Newbolt (1862–1938). Newbolt is best known for the line 'Play up! play up! and play the game', from his patriotic poem 'Vitaï Lampada' ('The Torch of Life'), written in 1892. The poem tells how a schoolboy learns about devotion to duty while playing cricket, and later applies this same selfless attitude to the battlefield.

2 By the time the war was over, it had claimed the lives of fifty-seven of the school's old collegians. Gratton House, named for the school's founding headmaster, was built and dedicated to their memory.

Acknowledgments

I must first of all thank my uncle, David Murrie, for his support of this book which honours the life of his older brother and places it in the context of our family. He gave me a detailed and most informative summary of Glen's life, copied photographs for me, and provided an impressively complete family tree showing the myriad connections between the Murries, the Inglises, the Murrays, the Logans, the Shannons and the Vigars. Without this document at hand I would have been hopelessly at sea. His reminiscences and memories were also very helpful, as were those of Bruce Murrie, his twin, and Gwenyth Lodge, his sister. I am especially indebted to Gwenyth for lending me Nancy's photograph album, Glen's letters to his parents and his 'Flighing Dairy', and the many letters relating to Glen's death. Without these very moving primary sources the book would be considerably poorer.

My thanks, too, to my immediate family for their support and encouragement, and particularly to my cousin and fellow writer Vivienne Kelly for her unfailingly generous help and advice.

I thank the Australian National Archives for giving me permission to quote from service records held by them, and the No. 22 (City of Sydney) Squadron Association for allowing me to reproduce chunks of information from their Operations Records. In addition, I thank the very helpful staff of the Australian War Memorial Research Centre, who advised me on matters ranging from RAAF protocol to the internal layout of an A-20 Boston Bomber. I must also acknowledge Trove, the National Library of Australia's incomparable newspaper archive, from which I unearthed many fascinating bits of information simply unobtainable elsewhere, and Scotch College for lending me Glen's logbook, which is held in their archive. I am grateful to Peter Trumble, former archivist at Scotch College, for researching details of Glen's time at the school.

Finally, I thank the family of Nancy Griffith (Priddle) for their generosity in allowing me to write about her life and to reproduce the letters she wrote to Glen's family after his death. The story of Glen and Nancy mirrors the sort of tragedy experienced by thousands of couples and families as a result of war, and it is at the heart of this book. Sydney and Ian Griffith, and Ian's wife Janet, have been most helpful in telling me more about Nancy and the Priddles, making old photographs available to me, and correcting my inevitable errors.

And to Glen Murrie, the third brother, the man in the photograph: you never knew me, but I am Aunt Em and Uncle Will's granddaughter, Len's daughter, David and Elizabeth's niece. I am so proud that we have a family connection. It has been a privilege to tell your story.

Index

Page numbers in **bold** type refer to photographs.

N

S

T

U

V

Wakefield Press is an independent publishing and
distribution company based in Adelaide, South Australia.
We love good stories and publish beautiful books.
To see our full range of books, please visit our website at
www.wakefieldpress.com.au
where all titles are available for purchase.

Find us!

Twitter: www.twitter.com/wakefieldpress
Facebook: www.facebook.com/wakefield.press
Instagram: instagram.com/wakefieldpress

Printed in Australia
AUOC02n0835021117
291121AU00014B/14/P

9 781743 054253